always Carl

Letters from the heart and heartland

1929-1931

Amy McVay Abbott

Dedication

In Honor of Donna Enz Argon

and

In Loving Memory of

Carl August Enz

1899 – 1983

ISBN: 9781099183584

Imprint: Independently Published

First edition August 2019
Index added 8/23/2019

Cover design and book graphics by

Diana Ani Stokely, grafixtogo.com, Hamilton, Texas

1931 photograph used on the cover

Perrey Studio, Fort Wayne, Indiana

Carl Enz is pictured on the back cover with his Purdue key in his pocket, in the mid-1920s.

Table of Contents

Always Carl

Introduction

This book shares the intimate 90-year-old letters of a young man, Carl August Enz, who was my maternal grandfather. My aunt, Donna Enz Argon, gave me a stack of letters from my grandfather to my grandmother LeNore Hoard Enz, valuable documents written almost a century ago. I promised to copy the papers for my cousins. While I am not fulfilling the letter of the law, this project should suffice in spirit.

The letters were written during Carl's travels as a field man for two farm management companies. His wife, Alma Mahler, died tragically after the birth of their only daughter, my Aunt Donna, in 1928. Carl courted a young nurse, LeNore, and these letters recorded his thoughts, fears, hopes, and dreams.

After a death, most people lionize their loved one. That is not the purpose of this book. I loved my grandfather dearly, and he was a good man. Yet, each of us has flaws, biases, and weaknesses interspersed with our good qualities. Our complicated emotional lives are what make us human. These letters give us a window into the young man's soul. Carl is ambitious, witty, dedicated, kind, and influential. We also see sarcasm, jealousy, bias, and even fear at this challenging time. He longs for more time with his infant daughter and deals with terrible grief as he mourns his deceased wife.

To read his words is a gift to us. To read his words at the most poignant time in his life, when our family, as we know it today was founded, is a gift to us. To learn about his intense pain and witness his ability to survive a tragic situation is a gift to us. We have the advantage of hindsight, and we know the end of his story. We know he lived well and built a successful home and family. He helped others through his business, his church, and his civic engagement.

The letters are in cursive writing or typed on hotel or company stationery from all over Carl's sales territory, primarily in Indiana and Illinois. The letters begin in late 1929 and continue until shortly before Carl's April 12, 1931, marriage to my grandmother, his second wife, LeNore Hoard.

The book title comes from his signature, "Always Carl" (without a comma). "Always" was his choice word, but another frequent signature was his full name, Carl A. Enz. Even months before their wedding, he signed Carl A. Enz. One letter is signed "Your future bed pardner, Carl A. Enz" and another, "Yours for success." Intimacy and formality, in one package.

I corrected most spelling and grammatical errors unless it was part of the context *(see "pardner" above)*. Where I could provide context, I added a footnote. Duplicate letters or those that added no new information were eliminated.

I've added several original letters and envelopes as illustrations. The letterhead itself tells a story, recalling an era of classic Art Deco styling. I've also included information about the world beyond the windshield of a Midwestern field man's automobile.

Most of the letters were written or typed on hotel letterhead, and information on the only surviving property, the Severin in Indianapolis, is included.

There is an extensive gallery of photos from the Mahler, Enz, and Hoard families. Prose and pictures together tell the story of a young man on his way up in the world.

My information comes from oral history, family documents, and continuing research, as well as personal communications given to me by my late grandmother LeNore Enz and my aunt, Donna Argon. The story ends in Springfield, Illinois; their lives beyond the early 1930s is for another time.

Carl Enz died in 1983. This August will mark 120 years since his birth on an Indiana farm and is an appropriate time to publish his letters. Curating his words from ninety years ago has been an extraordinary journey for his granddaughter.

Amy (LeNore) McVay Abbott
Newburgh, Indiana
August 2, 2019

Always Carl

Carl August Enz Biography

Carl August Enz was born to Charles Amiel Enz and Augusta Hannaman Enz in White County, Indiana on August 2, 1899, the second of three children. He joined an older sister, Edith Marie. Later, Walter Henry joined the family.

Charles and Augusta were born in White County as well. Charles' parents were George and Amalie Wiese Enz, both immigrants from Germany. Augusta's parents died of tuberculosis when Augusta was small. She and her sister Ida were farmed out to cousins in the Westphal (Westfall) family, and little is known about her early life. (Her recently uncovered baptismal certificate lists her parents as Carl August Hannmann and Friedrika Louise Westphal. Her 1950 death certificate spells her name as Hannaman.)

Charles and August moved their family to Marion, Ohio, in the early part of the 20th century. Family lore dictates that Charles felt frustrated when Indiana land taxes went up to $1 per acre, so he moved the family.

Carl attended school in Marion County, Ohio, and was proficient with school debate and agriculture contests. An article from *The Marion Daily Star*, March 9, 1916, notes that Carl Enz participated with Morral High School on the debating team. The topic for that year, likely his junior or senior year in high school was, "Resolved, that the United States Army and Navy should be strengthened."

The *Fort Wayne Daily News* notes that the Enz family moved back to Indiana in the fall of 1917 to Jasper County near the village of DeMotte.

According to a letter to the author from Donna Argon, dated March 26, 2009. "Carl attended the highly-regarded Winter Short Course at Purdue and did very well. That put him in a top spot for a position with Straus Brothers where Carl's father Charles Enz worked."

Carl received honors in livestock judging at Purdue University, which would be repeated by his grandson Andrew McVay 50 years later at Purdue.

Donna Argon shared another nugget in her 2009 letter to the author, "Did you know that Charles Enz promised each son $1000 if they would not smoke before they were age

21?" Neither Carl nor Walter smoked, and both collected their rewards. We know that Carl spent some of his on a car.

He may have donated some of the money to Purdue University for the building of the Purdue Memorial Union. The building was dedicated to those who lost their lives in "The War to End All Wars." Groundbreaking on the building was during Homecoming in fall 1922.[1] Donna pointed out that because of Carl's success in the Purdue Winter Course, he was able to land a job with Straus Brothers and defer his service. Carl's name is engraved on a plaque that remains today at the PMU.

Carl's brother Walter attended Valparaiso University in northwestern Indiana.

Walter was a bright and engaging young man, handsome with a beautiful smile. Carl told tales of how the two brothers crashed random family reunions, pretending to be relatives, for a free meal. Both always dressed impeccably; did they charm everyone at the party?

Walter met a young woman at inter-fraternity dances named Alma Mahler, a co-ed who came to Valpo from the western part of Kansas. Walter thought his brother, Carl, and Alma might hit it off and introduced them.

Precious items saved by Donna reveal Alma's life well lived at Valpo. President of her sorority, Alma was active on campus and popular with her peers. A dance card from Alma's college days had ten slots for her dance partners to sign. The saved one recorded six[2] signatures of Carl Enz (five of which he signed Carl A. Enz).

---

[1] https://union.purdue.edu/home/about/Index.html

[2] Look closely at the signatures. Did Carl dance every dance with Alma? #7 and the second extra appear to be made up names. Fudeskerdinker? Gessbudler? All the "Ws" seem identical. Suspicious?

Alma Mahler was born in 1905 to Adolph Mahler and Mathilda "Tillie" Emilie Strickert Mahler. Adolph was an upstanding farmer and bank director. The Mahlers and the Strickerts came to Kansas in the nineteenth century. Adolph died when Alma was a child, and Tillie focused her efforts on getting Alma the best education available. Tillie married Fred Mahler, a cousin of her late husband.

The *Lafayette Journal and Courier* reported of the young couple's Kansas wedding on July 6, 1927. "Announcement is made of the marriage of Miss Alma Mahler of Scott City, Kan., and Carl Enz, of Fort Wayne. The ceremony took place July 6, at the home of the bride's parents, Mr. and Mrs. F. H. Mahler, in Scott City. Mr. Enz attended Purdue University and is employed as a field man for the Straus Brothers company. Mrs. Enz, after receiving her early education in Scott City, attended Valparaiso University. She is a member of the Sigma Theta sorority of which organization she was president during the past year."

The couple settled into their Fort Wayne home several miles from Carl's parents who lived at 1821 Alabama Avenue. Alma became pregnant with their only child, Donna, who was delivered by Caesarian section on September 21, 1928, at the Lutheran Hospital in Fort Wayne.

Two hours after the baby's birth, 23-year-old Alma passed away. The death of a young mother during a hospital birth was a highly unusual event. The Centers for Disease Control keep mortality statistics, and of 1000 live births in 1928, seven resulted in the mother's death.[3]

The baby was given the full baptismal name of Alma Donna Ruth Enz.

Alma's death was unexpected and horrifying, to say the least. And forever tragic for her widowed mother hundreds of miles away in Kansas, her young husband, and of course, the baby who would never know her mother.

---

[2]https://www.cdc.gov/nchs/data/vsushistorical/mortstatsh_1928.pdf

LeNore Alice Hoard Biography

LeNore Alice Hoard was the third child of Henry Kellis Hoard and Anna Long Hoard, born on the family farm in Washington Township, Whitley County, Indiana, on June 28, 1908.

LeNore's father was involved in community activities, having served in many agriculture organizations, including the fair board and Farm Bureau. He also served as chairman of the Booster committee for the South Whitley Fair in the teens and twenties, and similar festivals continues today.

LeNore's oldest sister, Zoe Hoard (wearing a black hat), with her friends at the South Whitley Fair. Zoe is driving her grandfather Washington Long's car.

LeNore's mother was the daughter of Washington Long, a farmer, the son of Reuben Long, who arrived in Whitley County in 1837. Her mother was Mary Jane Baker, daughter of Jonas Baker, an early pioneer. Anna inherited the Reuben Long 160-acre farm from her father.

LeNore's father was the son of John Tyler Hoard and Catherine Creager Hoard. "Kate" Creager's grandfather, Peter Creager, was an early settler of South Whitley, Indiana, and helped build the main street, State Street, that remains today. Peter and his family arrived in the late fall of 1836.

Both LeNore's sisters, Zoe and May, took teacher training after high school. May Hoard died in a car accident in Allen County, Indiana in July 1922 when she was 20. LeNore was 12 when her beloved sister died.

LeNore was a good athlete at Washington Center High School, playing on the girls' basketball team and making the honor roll. Her high school basketball team won the county championship in 1926.

After high school, she attended the Registered Nurse training program at Lutheran Hospital in Fort Wayne. As a student nurse working in surgery, LeNore was present on September 21, 1928, when Donna Enz was born and Alma Enz passed away.

After graduating from nursing school in 1929, LeNore worked as a traveling nurse, sometimes at the hospital and often in private homes.

Baby Donna and her father, Carl, 1928.

New Hotel Plum
Streator IL
October 14, 1929
Dear LeNore:

I feel somewhat guilty in asking you for a date, after being called away, neglecting you, not calling you or sending you a wire. Sunday has been my only chance home, and in the morning, I went to church. In the afternoon, the neighbors came over, and until four o'clock, we were kept at home.

There, immediately after, we took the baby out for a ride, and then I went up to see you at the hospital. My not finding you was a disappointment to me and so I went back home. A neighbor came over, and this made just enough people to play cards. You can easily see how hard it would be to get away and leave our company. Then, too, the baby had been sick, and Mother was ill during the week, and Father asked me to stay and help care for my baby.

You know, when Father says "stay," he usually means every word. LeNore, I am really very sorry that I caused you this disappointment. But, about the only thing I can do is call you after I get home. I am planning on coming back on Saturday.

Mrs. John Whaley said she will meet me at the Wilson farm near Peoria on Monday morning, which means that I can't drive home and get back here on Monday morning. My work is much like yours in that respect. How can we ever see a show? My brother-in-law bought a new Buick sedan, and I had planned on showing it to you yesterday.

I only have a few more farms to rent, and that part of the work will be done. I hope someday to enjoy a good show with you and maybe another good long ride if you don't object. I wish we could be together at Fort Wayne tonight.

Sincerely, Carl A. Enz

Princeton, Illinois
October 23, 1929
Dear LeNore:

I received your big fat letter this morning at Peoria. Mr. and Mrs. John Whaley met me at the Mayer Hotel on Monday evening and finished our work on the Wilson 760 acres on Tuesday. This morning we drove to Bloomington and purchased paint and decided to paint all the buildings on the farm.

Here we parted, and they drove to Ohio, and I drove over here to Princeton, Illinois. Today was undoubtedly terrible to operate, f or the snow was coming down hard and fast and sticking on the windshield. The snow is about three inches deep here tonight and very cold. My room is too cold to sit and write letters, so I have moved to the lobby.

I am coming home over the weekend and can see you either Saturday or Sunday evening unless my car is wrecked before I go home. Mother and sister and brother-in-law[4] are going to Reynolds over the weekend, and Donna and I will take care of ourselves. You had better come over and join the crowd; maybe I can arrange this visit.

My tooth is causing some trouble this evening, and the freezing weather isn't helping. The mud roads are terrible here. Remember, LeNore, I'm calling on Saturday evening and making plans. We have plenty to talk about

Always Carl

---

[4] Sister Edith Enz Hipsher and brother-in-law Quincy Hipsher

(margin top, upside down) Good bye old Queen! (Words fail to express etc.)

Carl Enz

Nov. 5 1929
VALPARAISO, IN.

Dear LeNore :—

Arrived at Valpo at 7 o'clock this evening no supper and mighty tired. Drove all day trying to buy figs and made a complete failure.

Left Alma Donna Ruth just feeling fine and waving her hand bye bye as I drove away. Ate dinner at South Bend and thought by chance maybe I could see your Sister because of it being noon. but on account of the rains everyone stayed in shelter.

Very cold here this evening. Left a call for 5 o'clock in the morning. Boy how I wish I could change it to 8 o'clock. Driving to Quincy Illinois tomorrow if possible.

Well — now — are you still holding the old man's hands. Ha. Getting several pictures finished so you can have one and then to Mrs Mahler would like several.

Very anxious to get to Peoria for the two letters.

Going to bed right now (Hear me snore) Ha.

Sincerely

This is the Moon.

Carl Enz

(left margin) (always watch when you have eggs in pocket) (Never fall with a cake) (I am The Queen)

Those bright lights:

(right margin) The Rector is working fine. (Where do we go? Sheldon) (I am The Queen)

Letters from the heart and heartland, 1929-1931

Lafayette Hotel
Rockford, Illinois
November 11, 1929
Dear LeNore:

Arrived here at about six o'clock this evening and tired of riding. The boys at the office wired me to meet them at Janesville, Wisconsin, on Tuesday evening. I plan on working near here tomorrow morning and then driving to Janesville tomorrow afternoon. Today was undoubtedly one pleasant day to travel.

The Ford, with the nice green color, is changing slightly to the stucco mud finish. Sure glad that I had the Ford washed so you could see the new green paint.

This is one nice city in Illinois and is widely known for business transactions.

My business will be to pay for the room. Ha. <u>Breakfast, Dinner, and Supper!</u> Three times a day, let us get fat! Ha!

What did your helper say when you came in so late? I was just wondering if I got the blame or the green Ford? I can imagine hearing Dollar and Cents at Convoy[5] saying to Mike, *do you suppose Carl caused LeNore's dress to be torn?*

Notice at a garage in Aurora, Illinois. "The world is coming to an end. Pay your bills now – so – we won't have to look all over – HELL – for you." Ha!

Today was one long lonesome drive for me, sure wish you could help care for one of the company's field men or become a private nurse for me.

I am not so sure about going to South Bend[6] since the boys are one day late on the trip.

This is not Saturday night, but the opportunity has presented itself now for one more bath and plenty of sleep tonight. Do hope your next case will be in the daytime so we can step out to a show, say, at South Whitley or Zulu. Maybe Convoy? Who knows?

---

[5] A reference to the nurses with whom LeNore lives.
[6] South Bend is the home of LeNore's sister Zoe Hoard.

Always Carl

Sending a few snapshots and the latest pictures will be posted later. All the folks were well except little Donna Ruth, and her cold was much better.

Unless the boys keep me going to Michigan, I will drop you a note from Wisconsin.

Bye, bye, dear, Carl

Hotel Orlando
Decatur, Illinois
November 20, 1929
Dear LeNore:

Your big fat letter came just as I was leaving the hotel at Peoria. Everything has gone well this week except on Wednesday at New Carlisle where the snow was 15 inches deep in the wheat field on the levee. We tried to work and soon found that most of our time would be spent in trying to get out of some lousy hole that was covered with snow and could not be seen.

Drove over to Peoria and got within five miles of the place when something went wrong on the transmission of my car. I drove in low gear to Peoria. Arrived safe but late for supper. Went to bed mighty early for you gave me instructions to take good care of my cold and save it for Sunday evening. Called my tenants and had them come in to see me while the Ford was being repaired. The bolt came loose in the line shaft and almost came disconnected, leaving the rear running gears falling out and almost causing an accident again. This was certainly one close call to another crash. Enough said this time.

You can imagine how well I like to receive your big fat letters. Your special message was awaiting me at Peoria. No snow south of Valpo. Mighty cold here this evening and prospects of getting much colder. Take good care of Donna[7] and be careful of Daddy for he is rated high. Did he see us driving around the block?????

Called Zoie and had a pleasant visit but on account of the terrible snowstorm really felt it better for both of us to stay in and care for our colds. Zoie said that she would write to you. Hope you are feeling well again and can arrange to be at Fort Wayne on Sunday of the week. Wondering this evening about Donna Ruth. Now, let us drive around one more time. Let them look (who cares)! Ha.

Bye, bye,

Always Carl

---

[7] What does Carl mean here? Did LeNore do private duty nursing for the Enz family? There is no additional information. The "Daddy" here may be Charles.

Always Carl

Hotel Jefferson
South Bend, Indiana
November 23, 1929
Dear LeNore:

Just 11:30 p.m. when I left your older sister at her little home on 802 North Lafayette.[8] After delivering the evening dress, I received an invitation for a visit.

We had a lovely visit, and your name was mentioned several times! We talked about your case in Convoy, Ohio, and that you said you were going to California. Zoie said, "Do you believe she really means it, because if so, I would worry myself over it."

She is sure worried over your trip to Convoy and the great danger of contracting the disease.[9] Sure feel guilty in stopping after hearing about the unfortunate case you had at the time.

My Ford broke down before I left town this morning and I was at the garage until two o'clock when I drove to South Bend.

You asked me to stay up with Zoie until quite late, and 11:30 p.m. is sure late for her now. What am I do to do next? Ha.

You said you would tell me the news later, so I am waiting patiently. Hope you are feeling well, dear, and have good success with your patient.

Bye, dear

Always Carl

---

[8] Current site of South Bend YMCA.
[9] LeNore cared for several tuberculosis patients.

Carl Enz, Fort Wayne, Indiana, 1929

Always Carl

December 2, 1929

Dear LeNore:

Just called up your <u>older</u> sister and told her about your experiences and consulted her on several other matters, weather, for instance. Ha.

Drove down here today and got stuck at Goshen in a deep snow drift, finally got out and experienced several more drifts before retiring for the day. The snow is mighty deep here in South Bend and on our farm. The lane to the farm is all drifted shut and deep in places.

Tried hard to finish the work here today but I guess one just can't get ahead in these times. The Ford is running fine, and the heater is doing much better. The chains may last until tomorrow and then a new pair, all in one week. Just had a good warm bath and now I can hardly keep my eyes open to write. My room is mighty comfortable, warm, and cozy.

How is your patient?[10] Sure hope that he can recover soon for he sure worries me because it was my fault for taking you away. I am the unluckiest man in the world for everything that I do always has this kind of an ending. Something always happens, and then I regret having caused you so much trouble already.

You failed to ask about Donna Ruth. She is certainly feeling fine and going everywhere and keeping someone busy after her. Soon she will be talking, and then Dad can hear aplenty. Soon must buy some Christmas presents for her and play Santa Claus.

Well, you are right. We are going to a show next time I come home. Dear—be careful about lifting and get enough sleep.

Bye, dear

Always Carl

---

[10] A patient became worse after LeNore took a break from his care.

Valparaiso, Indiana
December 4, 1929
Dear LeNore:

Now at the hotel at Valpo, waiting for my room to get warm. Boy, how cold it is here this evening. Someone said three degrees below, and I really believe it is true.

Drove for the past few days in and out of snow drifts and one barn lot after another and saw one face after another, some smiling and some not smiling. *My wife said that I should not sell the shoats. I must go up and see my wife.* Ha! Who needs the pigs?

We need about 75 shoats today; *Well, I have two that I can sell* (so encouraging.) Ha. *I have a cow that I will sell you. Mr. Jones has 30 shoats[11] for sale, drive right down. This Mr. Jones, yes, he came to see your shoats, well, I am looking for some myself* (Wonderful news.)

Johnson is having a community sale this afternoon, has 100 shoats in sale bill. Drove 50 miles over there and found 10 shoats in the sale, too heavy for us. Wonderful work in the snow drifts. Mighty glad to be going south with the feeling that warm weather is in sight tomorrow.

Remember, they shoot people down there (in southern Illinois). Look for the headlines in the newspaper. Ha.

Do hope you have success with your Grandpapa. Try and get your necessary sleep for health is needed. Zoie is coming home over the weekend, so be ready for a lecture.

Wish that I could run over for a visit this evening and not be disturbed. Ha. One must take life as it is and enjoy it. Well, someday we can see a show at Fort Wayne and enjoy it. Can we? Sure enjoy the pictures of you. Bye, bye, dear

Nite, Carl

---

[11] A shoat is a newly weaned pig.

Always Carl

December 5, 1929

Dear LeNore:

Arrived here at Gorham, Illinois this morning. Went out to the ranch today and had several experiences that you will hear later. The ground is covered with snow, and the tenant said that this has been the coldest weather in 40 years for the time of year.

We traveled all day without one thing to eat. The ranch has 5,350 acres in it, and most of it is covered with timber. Timber rats have begun to eat our wood, and this causes me lots of trouble in finding them and grief in several different ways.

The tenant shot three quail while driving on a trip. <u>Breakfast</u>, quail!

Do hope you have caught up with your sleep for you were just about overcome from the lack of rest. Zoie asked me about you, and I told her the truth.

Wish I could see you and the shows next week, but my business is something like yours. When you are ready to go, I am out here.

One sure sees several stop signs during the day, and they bring back memories.

I am staying here tomorrow and maybe can arrange to be in Quincy for Sunday. Your letter was certainly appreciated and do hope that mine was received.

We are all sitting around the stove and all smoking except me and some fellows playing cards. This would undoubtedly make a good picture of the family fireside.

Sincerely,

Carl A. Enz

Hotel Franklin
Carbondale, Illinois
December 6, 1929
Dear LeNore:

Your second letter came here this afternoon, and I arrived this evening. Sure glad to hear from you for this is in the middle of a section instead of an 80-acre farm.

The ranch is just the same old place and just as wild a country and as worthless as can be. Two old people run the hotel here, we have been telling stories and visiting all evening.

After talking to several bankers in each town near here and the county agent and several old people that have lived here, still have the same ideas in mind on this place. Have talked to several about making a hunting reserve out of the ranch and it seems that everyone agrees but who has the money to go ahead.

Drove all day with the chains on and glad to for several were in the ditches on account of lack of chains. The ranch is 20 miles on a dirt road near the Mississippi River, and they say in the spring there are several weeks that no one can get out to go anyplace. Can you picture me staying in this kind of place?

Tomorrow morning I am starting for Quincy, Illinois, and going through St. Louis about noon. Wish you were along for this will be a nice trip.

The old man that you were caring for has passed his usefulness and is only waiting for his time so please don't feel bad on this case. His age tells the story.

Your letter certainly indicates your feelings, and I certainly feel the same, and since reading your letters can picture you at home. Sure wish that I could be home and cheer you, but now I must be contented in writing. Sure getting anxious about some word from home, Donna Ruth especially. Well, dear, please don't worry over the case. Wish I could see you tonight.

Bye dear

Always Carl A. Enz

Hotel Quincy
Quincy, Illinois
December 7, 1929
Dear LeNore:

Sure enough, lonesome here. Drove from Gorsham this morning. Had planned on staying longer but soon the rain began to come so freely. The mud road for 20 miles back to Murphysboro and a possible chance or staying for a week started to stare in me in the face.

My Ford soon started north and landed in St. Louis for dinner and Quincy for supper. The mud roads were terrible, but the chains finally got me on cement roads. Then

it began to get colder, and when I started over in Missouri, the roads were covered with ice and snow. Crossed the Mississippi River three times. By the time I got to Louisiana, Missouri, the ice had turned to snow and then on my way to Quincy, the snow was at least two inches deep. I saw one farm of ours this evening and decided I can come home sooner.

Called the folks this evening and found all of them well including my big daughter. The long-distance telephone call was "only" $2.50, just imagine for only three minutes. It sure was worth it to me for after one week away from Little Alma, and I am almost wild to be home.

Then again, there are other reasons. For instance, the care of the nurse.

Tomorrow—can you picture me away down here sitting in a chair with a newspaper in my hands and one-half asleep (daydreaming?) Several more fellows are doing the same thing and wondering just how to plan Thursday work to be home over Sunday.

Tomorrow afternoon will be spent on Christmas shopping for ideas. Ha! (Save your pennies!) Zoie may call you about it.

How was the candy? Smiley Drug Store recommended it very highly. Remember, candy is fattening, and your weight is 131¼ pounds. Ha! Eat plenty and weigh 150 pounds and I will like you just the same.

Wish that I could be home with you over Sunday. Zoie said that she was going back over the weekend and expected to see you at home.

No doubt the poor old man had to be called home sometime Friday for the letter gave me that impression. You certainly did your part to keep him here with us as you have and satisfied his relation.

Please don't worry for gray hairs come at hard times. I am just wondering what you will be doing next Saturday and Sunday and if we could, by chance, get to see a show and have an enjoyable visit. How well I wish for some luck for us.

I am sure getting caught up with sleep for 10 to bed and up at 7 a.m. as regular as a clock. Nice room with bath and believe me two baths for me, only $3.00 for the bed.

One certainly needs plenty of money on a two-week trip. Sure wish you could see the country that I passed through today. Came into the hotel this evening and asked for my mail (no mail). Sure disappointed for I sure expected one from you.

Well, dear, please don't go on duty until you are entirely rested if it takes until next Monday. Now – what do you think of my plans?

Bye dear

Always Carl

Always Carl

Quincy, Illinois
December 8, 1929
Dear LeNore:

Sunday evening and I have all the papers read and just about ready to go to eat. How nice it would be to have lunch with you. Better just run over! Ha!

Have gathered together a few clippings of the day that probably will interest you at some lonesome hour.... Will Rogers, our President, and the joke of my mustache.

Today has certainly been lonesome for me. Continually reading and a walk over town on ideas for Christmas shopping.

People are busy shopping early this year, in fact, most of the cities are crowded every day. Several towns near St. Louis were certainly jammed yesterday. Mostly, all were near the ten-cent store! Ha!

Wonder where you are this evening? And if by chance you went home. Sure wish that I could be home tonight and just around the corner.

Have you gathered up all your clothes for this cold weather? Zoie said that she needed some clothes. I invested last night in some new clothes, a pair of socks, undergarments, and a tie. How well I am going to look next Saturday!

This hotel is certainly one dead place on Sunday. Worse than an 80-acre field. Working south about 20 miles tomorrow and probably stay all night here tomorrow night and go to Middlecoff Hotel at Paxton, Illinois, for Friday evening.

Well, dear, how well I would like to see you this evening. Do hope you are feeling well and resting up over the 24-hour shift.

Sincerely,

Carl A. Enz

December 9, 1929
Dear LeNore:

What have I done now? No letter for almost a week and no chance to receive any until I get home. Of course, I realize that you are busy. I am just about one day ahead of my schedule.

Drove from Carthage, Illinois, to Dallas City, and then on to our farm at Peoria and later to the Hotel Mayer for the mail. I just got one letter from Father. The office even forgot me out here.

Then I drove to Bloomington and received 19 letters in answer to my blind ad in the newspaper on our farm for rent near here. *I see your ad, Mr. Advertiser. I see your ad and can give good references, my dad, mother, sister, and brother!* Ha.

Well, now—since my letters are all read, and contents noted. Gee—how I wish for a message from you and how much I was disappointed at Peoria.

Father wrote that Alma Donna Ruth was sitting in her rocker and smiling in as much to say, "Tell Daddy hello." Two long weeks out here in the mud is just too long.

Wonder where you are this evening? Suppose Zoie came home over Sunday and hope you got to see her.

Remember, dear, one hour later, Saturday night, to tell me the news that was to be in the letter. Ha! Sure hope for Saturday or Sunday night off, dear.

Nite, dear

Always Carl

December 10, 1929

Dear LeNore:

Now at Carthage, Illinois, awaiting dry weather and cold weather. This morning the roads were covered with ice, and then by 10 o'clock, the mud began. The chains were used all day, and no doubt will be used all day tomorrow unless we get colder weather.

Everything went smoothly today. And tomorrow I have all rent collections, and everyone needs the money. Stiff upper lip and hard-boiled eggs earn your salary.

Made special trip all day today in trying to meet the right road contractor on the new cement road going near our Ellis Farm. They are certainly right on passing the buck. I gave them all the devil to make sure that I would get the right one.

Your letter that was supposed to be at Quincy Hotel certainly did miss its calling for I made two trips to get the mail and you failed me sadly. This was one sad Carl, mighty blue for a letter.

Going to Peoria tomorrow but only to get the mail and continue to Bloomington to be near my work for the next day. Father sent a letter to me at Peoria telling me the news at home.

Wonder where you are this evening? No doubt you are on another case and will be unlucky enough to have all plans ready for the show, and then, well, you will be working. It all comes in a lifetime. To be with you and regardless of conditions means a lot to me, LeNore, awaiting the evening when we can be together again.

Sincerely,

Carl A. Enz

December 11, 1929
Hotel Orlando
Decatur, Illinois
Dear LeNore:

Now at the famous Orlando Hotel in high style. All I need here is money and plenty of it. Finally met a friend at an elevator and got a check cashed, so have enough funds to get home.

I am sure sick tonight for dinner at Springfield, Illinois, just put me under for the day. No supper and maybe no breakfast. If I only get well by tomorrow for the work must be done, and then, too, I had planned on seeing your uncle at Sheldon on Friday of this week.

All I need tonight is a nurse by the name of LeNore. Sure feel down in the mouth and sore in the tummy. It seems that travel and eating in a different place each day is not so good for me. Have lost 15 pounds in the last two weeks, one bad meal after another and soon one can notice the effects.

Tried to read the paper this evening but the bed seemed the best place under the circumstances. Toast and coffee for a while again. Also, a nurse when I get home.

Rain all day and a terrible fog this evening. The snow is melting, and the rain in this county sure has the roads and streets one mess of mud.

How I wish for a letter at Paxton on tomorrow evening. Gave a forwarding address at both places thinking you would write. Well, dear, what are you doing this evening? Have I been gone too long? Sure hope to be with you over the weekend.

Nite, dear

Sincerely,

Carl A. Enz

Always Carl

December 14, 1929
Dear LeNore:

Now at Bloomington, Illinois at the Arlington Hotel. Came from Dixon today and experienced another terrible day in the snow drifts. I saw several cars snowed under completely except about six inches of the top. I got stuck several times today but always had some man back of me that was in a terrible hurry. Ha. What luck for me.

Drove through the fields near LaSalle for about six miles, corn fields frantically all the way and mud about six inches deep. The cold spell came so suddenly and then, too, the ground isn't frozen to enable one to go everywhere in the fields.

How glad I am to be at this hotel tonight. Talked to another traveling man that stayed at El Paso last night and he said when he got up this morning, there were six inches of snow on the bed and floor. Boy, was he cold!

Over 80 cars stayed all night on the snow drifts between here and Peoria and two big busses just west of here about one mile. There were 20 cars snowed under completely.

Several places near here are drifted 10 feet deep on the main roads. Just imagine seeing me sitting out here, wondering just how long this blamed snow is going to last and how terrible it would be to get another storm in a few days and pen me in again.

This has been my first time to be stopped entirely from traveling in a car. Well, enough funds and suddenly here in this hotel is not so bad. How much nicer it would be to have you near to talk to and argue about the differences in daily tasks of life. Better come over tonight. *I can't, I am snowed in!* Now give me a good story and my comfortable chair.

Called the office a few minutes ago and related my experiences very satisfactorily. Well—my object was to come home but to my luck received an answer to stay here for the roads were just as bad there. Might just as well sit here as to be back. (Give me home, always.)

Must write to the folks and the office and then read the paper and go to bed. How nice it would be to go to Peoria for your letter. Maybe you can send them here soon enough.

Well, dear—where are you this evening? Working at the hospital or at home? How would I like to be home and drive over this evening for another enjoyable visit and be with my LeNore once again. Everything is upset now for I just can't tell you where I can be or will be. The roads are going to determine my trip.

Nite dear.

Your Carl

Christmas Card from Carl to LeNore, dated December 16,

and posted at Decatur, Illinois.

Hotel Lembke
Valparaiso, Ind.
Dec. 17, 1929
Dear LeNore:

Now at the above place and have a nice room and warm and cozy. Finished my work at the office and drove over to New Carlisle to our Gross Morris farm of 240 acres this afternoon. Then drove over here in the evening.

You can send my letters to the Mayer Hotel at Peoria until Friday and then send them to the Arlington Hotel at Bloomington, Illinois. Tuesday morning, I will be starting home, regardless of weather conditions.

Hotel Lembke
VALPARAISO, IND.

The Ford has delivered another rattle somewhere in front, so I am watching very carefully to avoid losing the motor. You know that the company may not approve of me driving it without a motor.

The folks were busy packing and wrapping boxes last night. Today I arranged to have a photographer come out and see our little girl for a few minutes. Do hope that she will take a good picture.

She was sure good today, and this made it so hard to leave her after all the fun together and then to see her wave bye-bye. She can do and understand so many things, and after all, is mighty smart and good.

My trip this week is mostly backward. Otherwise, I could give you specific information on my whereabouts at night.

I sure did feel guilty in calling you on Monday evening, but I guess after all – *"he is not so bad."* Going away for one week certainly should clear my title.

I know just how you feel toward me in coming to see you so much and then keeping you up so late, but dear, I can't help my faults. Now! Absolutely!

When you are near someone you like, well, the time seems to pass so fast. Then, too, your cases have kept us separated for several weeks.

I am sorry, dear.

Sure glad you liked the Christmas present for it means so much to me to know that everything is satisfactory (except Monday night. Ha Ha.)

Mayer Hotel in Peoria, Illinois, is the next place for me on the news. How much I look forward to your letters!

Wonder what your mother and father think of me? Well, I haven't used your father's car yet. Did the girls at the hospital see you and were you kidded?

Well, dear, Christmas is coming and so is Tuesday morning. Hope you have a case soon, but one for a few days. Mother asked me if you were going home for Christmas or if you could help us eat turkey.

Bye, Bye, dear

Always your Carl

Always Carl

December 20, 1929

Dear LeNore:

Came to Peoria today and received your letter here at the Mayer Hotel. Sure glad to be here and have your news. The snowstorm seems mighty generous in the section.

Do hope your case is a pleasant one this time and above all, has you free at Christmastime. You can picture me out here in the snowbound country looking east and wondering what is coming next.

The road to Peoria was open about 10 o'clock this morning, and I came through about noon. The snowbanks are just even with the top of the car and in some places much higher. Several of the big trucks are still in the snow drifts. Also, several cars are almost covered with snow, and in some cases frozen down.

How glad I am to be thoughtful enough to drive in early and avoid the hardships. Tonight leaves me here on Friday evening wondering just what to do. Can I get through tomorrow? Everyone tells me not to try for it is inhospitable.

Has Bookie milked old Spot lately? What does Dad think of your man? Is Zoie coming home with a man? Does "Old Henry" still have the transmission?

Now – called home and found everyone fine. How much I would feel to know about the road east.

Night dear

Your Carl

1929 History

The letters for 1929 end with this December note, and start again on January 9, 1930, after Carl has likely spent the holidays at home.

The year 1929 was significant in the history of our country.[12] Here are a few of the events of the year.

- ❖ According to "The People's History," the stock market bubble, which had been rising since the previous spring, burst on October 24, forever after known as "Black Thursday."
- ❖ The Philadelphia Athletics (not surprisingly) beat the Chicago Cubs four games to one in the World Series.
- ❖ New York's Museum of Modern Art (MOMA) opened on Fifth Avenue.
- ❖ The first Academy Awards, the Oscars, started on May 16th as a small event with about 300 people attending. Douglas Fairbanks, Sr., was the host of the 15-minute event.
- ❖ The U.S. population was 120 million.
- ❖ The first car radio was made by Motorola.
- ❖ London boasted the first public telephone booths.
- ❖ Famous people born in 1929 included Jacqueline Bouvier, Audrey Hepburn, Grace Kelly, and Anne Frank.

---

[12] What Happened In 1929 Including Pop Culture, Technology .., http://www.thepeoplehistory.com/1929.html (accessed June 11, 2019).

Letters from the heart and heartland, 1929-1931

Peoria, Illinois
January 9, 1930
Dear LeNore:

Well, you sure have the goods on me now. What must I say? Snowbound – yes. My plans are none. Streator was my next stop but oh the roads! Got stuck at Toulon and my only place to get shelter was here. The small town had no hotels, and now I am in Peoria.

Leaving tomorrow morning mighty early to get as near home as possible.

Selling corn and oats each day and settling cash rent occasionally. Nearly all the tenants are anxious to begin hauling grain.

The snow drifts are almost as bad here now as they were a few weeks ago. Today was a dandy for I was stuck more times than not. The Ford is running fine again and sure hope for success on my trip home. For my sweet little girl needs attention, and I must be the attention.

I finished reading the paper and will send a few jokes. The jokes you sent me are mighty witty. Some are very clever! Ha!

How I wish that I could drive out tonight and see you sitting up and the same good-natured smile that always greets me. *"Run on, Carlie, the company may fire you, and I do not want the blame!"*

Now, the girls sure have fun with me at the hospital, and I can picture seeing you trying to delay the conversation.

I have been thinking about my new work and new territory[13] How nice when you can go along to Indianapolis, Tipton and then to the state line at Sheldon.

---

[13] This reference must refer to Carl's switch from Straus Bros. to Prudential.

Also down to Tunker, Indiana, and then you can see the new tenants and get acquainted with all the children and at the same time get the stories that usually follow each visit.

It was sure getting cold here tonight. My throat is sore tonight, and my nurse so far away. Wait until I get home and then my nurse will be well and then some Beechnut gum and a pill and plenty of sleep.

Wonder where you are tonight, at home or at the hospital? Who knows? I am sending the mail to the hospital because I just felt that the sudden change of weather would keep you in the hospital.

I sure do miss the fountain pen this week. Next week will be mighty hard for me since my 30-days' notice will be up on January 15 and then I must give the company a notice to get another man in my place.

How I do hate to do this after being with the company for eight years here and eight years at the ranch (*Keener in Jasper County, Indiana, where his father Charles was the manager*) and Father has been with them for 25 years.

I am sure that Abe will feel bad and may hold this against me, but again, one must look out for himself in dollars and cents.

Now for a bath and good night's rest. Tomorrow will find me near my sweetheart. Wonder how Donna Ruth is tonight?

Dearie – if I only know how you were feeling. Something tells me you are not feeling so well. Saturday night, "Daddy" will drive out and see you. Regards to your folks. Take care of your health, dear. Nite, dear.

Your Carl

Always Carl

Valparaiso, Indiana
January 13, 1930
Dear LeNore:

Now at Valpo Hotel, supper surrounded, bed made, bath ready, and a letter to my dear one and then to sleep.

An adventure today for a tenant on one of our farms. Found the barn wholly burned to the ground and then his corn, oats, and hay also practically all his machinery went up in smoke. He got all the horses and cows out and the car.

The story as is, toast. The hired man left lantern sitting in the haymow and began work. The lantern fell over and fell to the bottom of the barn Soon, he had a good fire started. Now the barn is no more. The farmer had everything insured and will probably get $1300 out of a $500 investment. Not so bad. Enough said now on fires.

The hired man is scared to death and feels very guilty. I started your letter early, but Attorney Kelly came up for a visit and stayed for almost two hours. He has insurance on the buildings. We built a few air castles and decided that the world was all wrong. He has a farm, too, and says that money is scarce in that section.

He was sure surprised to hear of me leaving the company after so many years with Straus Bros. After I go with the new company, remind me and see that I get some of their business.

Guilty as can be after driving down to your place just at noon and sitting my big frame under the table and eating a three man's meal. I am almost as bad as the man who used a car, gas, and oil on several long trips.

Your dad and I can talk the business over with lots of enjoyment out of it. Not so much for you but get well as soon as you can and then we will have lots of things to talk about.

Future

1930 -1931

I don't believe that we should say anything to Roy or Zoe about naming their children for you know that Roy makes Zoe nervous.[14]

Zero weather in the morning, drove in the water and mud all day. Made fine connections today.

I imagine the neighbors are wondering what will be next. Get well and remember 150 lbs.

Nite, dear

Your Carl

---

[14] Roy remains a mystery, but Zoe married Everett Evans several years later.

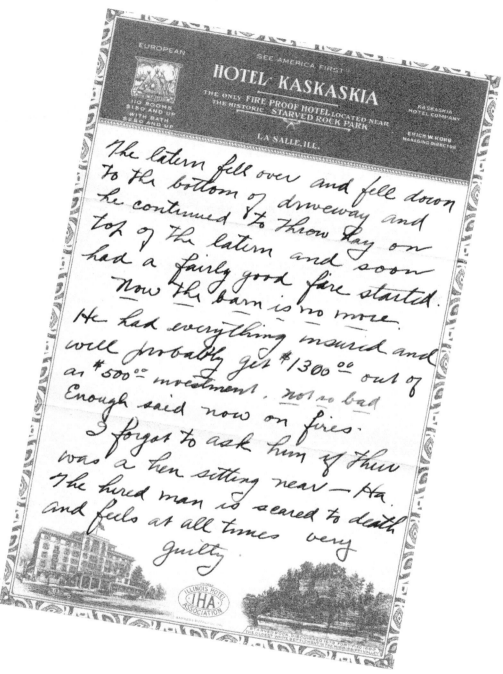

The latern fell over and fell down to the bottom of driveway and he continued to throw hay on top of the latern and soon had a fairly good fire started. Now the barn is no more.

He had everything insured and will probably get $1300.00 out of a $500.00 investment. not so bad Enough said now on fires.

I forgot to ask him if there was a hen sitting near — Ha. The hired man is scared to death and feels at all times very guilty.

Sample page of the previous letter. The letter was written at Valpo, but Carl must have saved paper from other hotels. The paper is intricate and lovely.

February 1, 1930
Vincennes, Indiana
Dear LeNore:

Now in the above place with 331 miles marked up on the Buick. Everything going fine and with all our worrying on the trip, the hotel certainly was congenial to be so patient.

No doubt your aunt was wondering just why I was in such a hurry, but one must be prompt in business. I am working tonight with a man from the main office.

We are going south to Kentucky tomorrow and finally work my way north by Saturday night.

This is certainly one grand country and fine friendly people.

Sold one farm today or rather have a proposition. Enjoy yourself while on the visit and remember 150 pounds before you stop.

Love, Carl

Always Carl

February 19, 1930
Dear LeNore:

Now at Washington, Indiana, for the evening and certainly one tired man. Walked three farms today and took several pictures and made several sales on grain.

The Buick is going strong but getting mighty muddy. Mighty warm here tonight. Worked steadily since 7:30 a.m. and now it is eleven o'clock p.m., and soon this boy will be in dreamland.

No doubt you have one grand time, for your folks. I am sure they will do their part to make you enjoy yourself. Remember you still have a few pounds to gain.

This is certainly one grand rolling country. The peach orchards are plentiful, so little Donna Ruth can rest assured that she can have peaches.

Just wondering, as usual, the number of dates you are having since your aunt made the statement. This made me feel rather strange for a few moments.

I may see you on Friday evening if the weather permits me to work. How much I would enjoy being with you tonight.

Always Carl

Marion, Indiana
March 3, 1930
Dear LeNore:

I just arrived at the Marion Hotel and have my little red wagon all loaded with the baggage and have begun to look around for someplace to sit this typewriter, so that I can write you a few lines before I hurt my finger.

You will notice that I use considerable shorthand in writing with this blamed thing. I feel rather good this evening in writing several of the tenants with this outfit and not making many mistakes.

The trip to Indianapolis was just a trip for nothing since the man was just a joke for he asked me to cash his check and I refused because I did not know him and then, too, I was short of money myself. He had a trip all planned for me to haul him around so he could finish some of his other work.

Donna Ruth was feeling so good this morning, and then I had to leave her so suddenly again and for so long a time. I sure hope that someday will find me at the head of some office so that I can be home with my little girlie in the many evenings to come. It was mighty hard to leave her this morning for she cried to go with me.

I filed my income tax report this morning before leaving town. I then drove to Indianapolis and got dinner and then drove to the Hamrick Farm to get the samples of soil. Also, to get my fill of this pest that came down to meet me from Chicago.

I sure hope you are getting more rest at the new place and can gain the 15 pounds and feel good again and be ready to go to work in the city by the time that I get back to good old Fort Wayne, Indiana.

I am afraid that the folks will persuade you to hire a new PORTER [15] The conversations usually bring on history and then being such good friends, I am mighty sure that someone will be down to see you while you are so handy.

---

[15] Porter was LeNore's former beau.

Always Carl

Mice will play in the absence of the cat, and I am sure that you were right in your statements to me last night. Now since we have this settled, and you have a date for Sunday, and I am working away here all by my lonesome, one just wonders sometimes whether it is better for you to have a good time since all I can do is work and try and be comfortable as times go on and on in life.

Your father is sore at me for the trips that I have given you and then, too, of us being together so much lately. I am sure that I have tried to show you a good time and certainly, I feel bad about making a failure of it.

Well, dear, I am going to bed with a very bad taste.

Nite, dear

Carl A. Enz

March 6, 1930

Dear LeNore:

Just arrived at Danville, Illinois, and have myself all set up in the Plaza Hotel and it is now 9:30 p.m. and I'm just getting started to work. I called McMahon at Fort Wayne and his brother at Georgetown, Illinois, this evening and I have my work all planned for tomorrow.

My work was certainly planned very satisfactorily, and the results are beyond question. I started at my aunt's house near Reynolds, Indiana, last night and failed to get any work done for they like to visit continually and stop my evening work. I didn't get to write the letter I had planned to write to you.

The Buick is doing its stuff, and how...today was one day for history as the rear tire picked up a spike, and the rest of the story is sad. The roads are horrible here, and one must use a lot of good judgment in driving especially in the new territory and then hunting the farms one usually drives down about all the bad roads in the community.

I realize that the steady work has begun to show on my weight, so I am letting down some on the speed of my work and trying to rest up a bit before I start working with the men in the badly run-down Illinois territory.

McMahon said that he would call the folks and tell them that I was still going strong. I am sure thinking of home and my little Donna Ruth this evening. And to think that one whole week more before I can come home to see my two girlies. Donna Ruth cried very hard when I left, and this certainly made it all the harder for me to leave.

Wonder where Porter will be over the week and how? Something tells me that everything is not so good for me since you have taken up the job in South Whitley and the way those people travel around and the chance for you to go with Porter. And your folks are such good friends, too. I am sure that they will be kind enough to invite him home to bring back the past.

Always Carl

Your letter that you agreed to send to Reynolds, Indiana, failed to come[16] and now I will be compelled to go the full two weeks without one single line from you. This, of course, always leaves a bad taste in my mouth.

Well, dear, I am doing my part in working, and you know what I am doing and in what state that I am working in and where. I have noticed a big change in you since we came back from your Aunt's and then your father gave me a hard look that was not necessary at the time.

HAVE A GOOD TIME, DEAR, FOR YOU ARE ONLY YOUNG ONCE, AND IT IS THE PRESENT TIME.

No more quarrels for me for I am acting natural from now on and no silence again.

Dear, your letters are always appreciated, and now I must go on working without one. I hope you are feeling better.

Nite dear

Carl

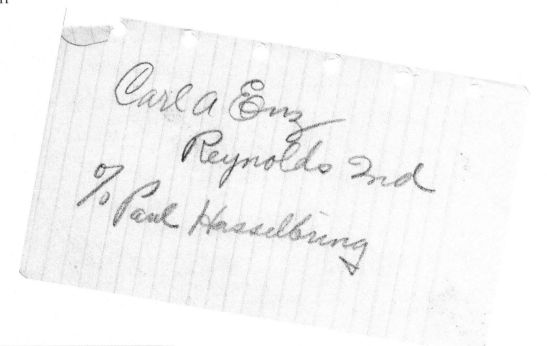

---

[16] Was the handwritten address slipped inside the letter a big hint for LeNore to write Carl?

HOTEL LAWRENCE

56 Rooms
30 Rooms—Tub Bath
10 Rooms—Shower Bath
All Rooms with Running Water

Operated By
Lawrenceville Hotel Company
P. B. McCULLOUGH, Pres.

A Fire-proof Hotel
in the heart
of the
Business District

Lawrenceville, Ill.,..193....

March 7 1930

Dear LeNore;

Now at the above place and one lonesome
man for it seems that I hav'nt a friend in the world
no mail and just work and no play gets mighty tire
some to me after a few days like this one.

Everything went well until I had ten
miles of mud road and then after I worked so hard and
got down to the farm , the tenant was gone and here
I was away out there and no place either.

Finally located the tenant and got the
requirements and drove away as soon as possible and
got down here for the evening. This is a mighty poor
Hotel but I guess that age has its day.

The Buick got real hot today in pulling
through the muddy roads. She is a great car for me
at this kind of work for I almost live in it.

You can send my mail in care of Wm.
McMahon at Georgetown Illinois and I will stop and
get it the last of next week on my way home. The
next few days will be undecided for me because the
Illinois man will decide my trip.

How well I would like to be home and
see both of my little girlies, providing that the
weeks absence has not made a change in the future
plans with one of my girlies. We know that this is
a fast age and one can hardly keep up with it .

I am pretty busy writing letters to a
the tenants informing them on the seeding of the
clover seed that I am buying now.

Hope you are feeling better and that
you have gained /----- well lets say 7 lbs. Can you
truthly say that you have gained the above amount.

I will write you a nice long letter
over the week end while you are enjoying your self
with the friends from South Whitley Indiana.

Call the folks while you are in the
city and find out all about my little girlie and
write me the news.

Enjoy yourself dear
Nite Nite

Carl A Enz.

Advertisement on the back of the hotel envelope.

March 9, 1930
Dear LeNore:

I just came in, and I have my work in shape, and although it is midnight, I felt I had to write you tonight because tomorrow will be another busy time of it and one just must be on your toes with this class of people.

Tomorrow will finish me up in this section and then for another land that will probably be in the western part of the state. Then I expect to go to Georgetown and get my mail and get started for home just as soon as possible for the closer I get home the more anxious that I get and the faster that I will be driving.

The Buick is still doing its stuff and getting many miles on it. I sure feel good to have such a good automobile away out here and know that soon I will be going home. Today I was just sick when I got into a bad place in the road and got down and was held up until I could get a team and get pulled out. Mud everywhere.

It is raining here this evening, and I have several farms to visit on mud roads but will not try them until the next day. Probably they will be dried off and in good shape by that time. This hotel is somewhat better than a barn but not very comfortable for a person as lonesome as me.

Sunday was certainly one long day for me, but I met Paul Funk, the seed corn king of the world and spent the afternoon with him and plan on seeing him again if possible. The Funks are very common and very nice people to talk and deal with.

My expenses were terrible this last week for they were just under the $100 and you can imagine me broke away down here in no man's land. Well, dear, take good care of yourself and gain the 20 lpounds. And then go to work but not before. Ha! Dear, I must go to bed – Nite, night, dear.

Always just,

Carl A. Enz

Always Carl

March 11, 1930
Dear LeNore:

No doubt you are wondering just where I am this evening, but I am going back north to Marion County, Illinois, and then over to Georgetown, Illinois, and get your letters and sit down and read over and over because the two weeks seem like years to me.

I have the southern section all finished and everything going smoothly again. The mud roads were fair in comparison with them after one of those heavy rains. I am just tired out and can hardly write, for the new men every day certainly give me chase over the farms.

Made several long settlements today and this, of course, is tiresome for me. The irregular meals are not helping me very much, and I am sure that I have lost several pounds lately.

No word from home for almost ten days, and I am about ready to start home anytime. The work out here is waiting all the time, but there will be some of it waiting for next week for this boy is going home on Saturday without fail.

Wonder how you are feeling and where you are tonight? There are so many thoughts going through my mind tonight, and no word from anyone for a long time.

Well, dear, enjoy yourself for the last week away is not a good one for me. Hope you are feeling better and can go stepping[17] again. I will be calling for you when I get home and try to locate you.

Nite, Nite, dear.

Carl A. Enz

---

[17] "Stepping" is an idiom of the 1920s meaning dancing and having a good time. Irving Berlin memorialized the phrase in the 1948 musical "Easter Parade," with Fred Astaire performing, "Stepping Out with my Baby."

March 21, 1930[18]
Dear LeNore:

How much I enjoyed your letter awaiting me here at the hotel. The last few days have been terrible for me because of the feeling that has been before me.

McMahon received a letter from the home office asking for a complete report on all grain sold and the 1930 crops and prospects. I began working on this the next day after I called you and kept continually at it until last night.

I am just tired out after such a terrible strain and so steady at only one thing.

The figures are always before me and tonight will be a good rest, and then Sunday will be another good day for rest.

I can picture you and the girls going to church on Sunday and the care about the place. Wonder just how the flowers are and if the girls have any more callers?

Well, dear, I am working hard to make a success and oversee an office soon, and then I can be home every night. How much I would like to be home over Sunday and see you and talk over our affair, which has certainly been a heartbreaker to me. I have always tried to make our trips a pleasure and be of help to you in times of need and enjoy your company. Maybe after you feel better and have more pep, you can appreciate me more at least I sure hope so, dear.

I will write you a long letter on Sunday after I call your Aunt down here.

Hope you are feeling better towards me. Always Carl

---

[18] Map copyright 1998 Encyclopedia Britannica, Inc.

Always Carl

March 25, 1930
Dear LeNore:

Down at the little town of Rockville, Indiana. They say it is going down to zero tonight and this hotel room seems like it is much lower! The last few days have been terrible for me to get to the farm because of the rainy weather and the bad roads.

I am getting mighty good results and doing lots of work considering the weather and roads.

Wonder what you are doing this evening and just where you are and if you are back at our own dear city? How much I would enjoy a letter but must be contented until I get back to Indianapolis.

The two weeks seem like years to me after being home at least once a week. I sure hope that I can be lucky enough to get a job sometime that will keep me home with my dear little girlie.

Tomorrow I am meeting the big man from the little town and going over the loans that we are soon getting. This is mighty nice work, and one certainly enjoys talking to these men.

Well, dear, these few lines will let you know where I am and how I feel, and that is about all. I am just so tired out this evening that I hardly know what I am writing and where I am currently. Well, dear, bye. Enjoy yourself.

Always Carl

March 31, 1930
Dear LeNore:

Now at the little hotel in Greencastle, Indiana, and mighty tired and lonesome. I failed to sleep last night and then drove down here and surveyed the 600 acres south of Indianapolis. I had planned on going south but got tired and put up for the night.

I am just tired out completely and then came the news that you told me. Then leaving both you and the baby and working down here for the full two weeks has me just about worried sick. It just seems to me that everything I do is wrong, and then I am compelled to go away without an understanding.

The past two years have brought on more gray hairs, and it seems like the next few years will make them all gray. I am working continually and saving my money and trying to have a home that will be happy and enjoyable for the one that shares it with me. But it seems that people now only look at the present.

I am sending this letter to your home for you said that you were going home, and this will work out okay. You must be careful and not get wild again for it certainly shows poor judgment in the thoughts that are in your mind.

Well, dear, I am working and working. This is all for someone because I don't enjoy being away from home and working so hard. I think that you should have more confidence in me, and your thoughts will not run so wild. Hope you are feeling better and found the time to call the folks and write me a few lines.

Just Carl

Always Carl

Utley Hotel
Mount Vernon, Indiana
April 1, 1930
Dear LeNore:

I wish that you would look on the Indiana map [19] and try and locate me and see for yourself, the miles before me, and the ones that I leave behind.

Tonight finds me here, and tomorrow I will make three loan inspections and arrive at the Grand Hotel, Vincennes, and later to Buzan & Hastings at Washington, Indiana, where I am looking for your mail that must be there to satisfy one lonesome man.

Wonder where you are this evening and what you are doing. I am feeling much better this evening and have several hours work on the reports before I can go to bed. I suppose Zoe came down for a visit.

Hope that you and Zoe can find time to go and see my girlie. How I miss her away down here. Well, dearie, remember that I am coming back just as soon as I can and hope that they call me by Saturday. Do not worry, dear, and enjoy yourself.

Always Carl

---

[19] Map copyright 1998 Encyclopedia Britannica, Inc.

Washington, Indiana
April 4, 1930
Dear LeNore:

Away down here and Sunday coming and no decent place in view for me to stay. At this time I have no idea where I will be. Yesterday was a terrible day and not so very good results since the farms are so very hard to rent at this time. Nearly everyone that farms is well started and has their oats in and do not care to move. I am waiting on a man who is interested in renting this farm and sure hope that he can come clean and rent the place.

The sun is coming out nicely, and prospects could look bright. Everyone is busy thinking that summer is here. Now for a big drive tomorrow and a chance to make more money.

I will go to Vincennes this evening and work tomorrow morning. Then I will drive to our farm at Sullivan and finish what I can tomorrow and then probably go one step closer to Indianapolis. Then I can get my mail and feel that I am one step closer to home.

The inspections are mighty hard to make since this is a new country, and I am required to ask every question and then re-write the whole thing over on this blamed thing.[20]

The Buick is surely doing its stuff and every day. I've driven more than a thousand miles this week and prospects of more next week since the farms are scattered so badly.

I talked to McMahon yesterday, and he thought that I was going to Illinois this week and I sure informed him that I was going back toward Fort Wayne for next weekend.

I fully realize that there is a terrible lot of work to do but let them hire another man in the Illinois territory for I am only good for so much and that is all I can do at the present time.

Called the folks and found my little girlie doing just fine and getting her required sleep. She has begun to realize some about the time I am going to leave and follows me around to be sure to bid me goodbye.

---

[20] His typewriter.

Always Carl

I hope you are feeling well and enjoyed having your sister around. I hope you have talked about everything so that you can both go on with a full understanding of each other, and the folks at home.

One never realizes it, but we all know that our folks will not be with us that long, and it is up to us to help them appreciate the everyday happenings around them.

Your letter came to me last night and believe me it sure came at a good time when I was just able to see out, and that was about all. After one works continually for several days and has about everything happening, you certainly ask what is all about?

Well, dear, I must get busy and make my day out and mail your letter and go to the Post Office and see my results for the ad that I put in two newspapers.

Dear, I will be thinking of you on the long day of Sunday.

Bye dear, Enjoy yourself.

Always Carl

Vincennes, Indiana
April 6, 1930
Dear LeNore:

Just got back from one of our new farms that we are acquiring sometime in June, north of a little town by the name of Bicknell, Indiana. Found the tenant at home and we spent considerable time going over the place since I had nothing else to do but pass the time of day.

Worked on all my reports all forenoon and got them finished at noon, and then made the trip to Bicknell this afternoon. I just finished the report on the just inspected farm. I am glad to have my work completed as it worries me to have so many things to do.

Today is certainly a good day for people to get out and drive in the country. I guess every old trap is getting out today for exercise for they were well represented on the main roads. I got the Buick washed and then greased, and she looks like a new one. The clay mud had it in such a terrible condition that I thought I should have it washed before greasing.

Took pictures of the buildings on the farm today and feel sure that they will be good for the sun has been bright all day.

I ordered frog legs and sat there calmly waiting on the big feed. Soon the frog came along. It tasted good until toward the last. I began to look more closely and discovered that this frog had pin feathers. Of course, knowing something about the frog family, I realized I had discovered something new and profitable.

I wrote Mrs. Mahler[21] and intended on sending her a picture of my little girlie but forgot to enclose it in the letter. Something is working on me today as it seems I can forget so easily.

How much I would like to be at the Terre Haute House this evening and get your good letter that is waiting for me there. I will be there late in the evening, and then get the news that I long for and enjoy so much. My work is always more enjoyable when I start home, even going in the right direction helps. I am trying hard to finish all the work as I go and

---

[21] Mrs. Mahler is Donna Enz's grandmother, who lived in Scott City, Kansas.

then my next trip can be enjoyed much more, and I can spend more time on the loan inspection work.

Well, dear, I wonder where you are this evening, and what you are doing to entertain yourself. Work and letter writing is my work, for every Sunday that I am away from home. I certainly sent a big flock of letters to the office with my inspections for last week.

Hope your father is feeling better as he did look bad while we were there last Sunday. No more frog legs for me! Write to you from the Terre Haute House hotel tomorrow evening. Bye bye dear, one more week.

Always

Carl A. Enz

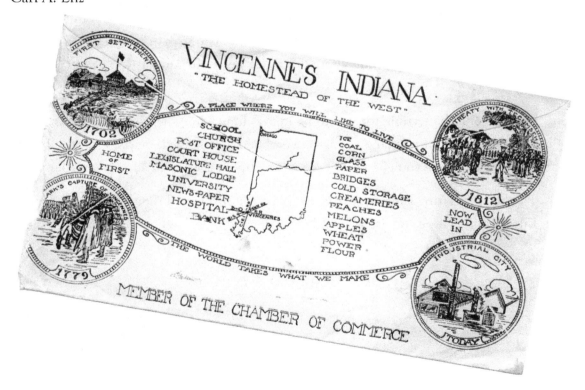

April 7, 1930
Dear LeNore:

Now at the little town of Rockville, Indiana, getting my day's work completed. I just finished this very minute, and it is 11 o'clock. I came through Terre Haute today, and sure enough, your two letters were waiting for me. I was getting low, and the letters sure gave me the pep again.

I think that I will need a nurse by the time I get home for the walking is terrible on these new shoes. They have begun to hurt my feet. I think if they continue to hurt me, I will have to buy a new pair and take this pair back. I have had several shoe men look at them, and they say that it is the fault of the shoe.

Drove over 250 miles today and feel rather good, considering the amount of work I've done. Every day is getting me closer, and who knows better than I do? I can see myself going home next Saturday morning about 50 miles per hour, and I don't mean maybe, either.[22]

It sure would be terrible for you to be idle so long while I am away and then about the time I came home to find you on a big case and tied down. Well, maybe you can take my sore foot as a case. I hope you got a case because the hours get mighty lonesome when idle.

The hour is getting late, and I have a big day tomorrow and then several bad days on and on through life. Hope you are well and busy.

Sincerely,

Carl

---

[22] Speed limits didn't come into wide use until the interstate highway system was completed in the 1950s. An average speed limit in the 1930s was 30 to 35 mph. https://www.sporcle.com/blog/2017/04/a-history-of-speed-limits/

Always Carl

Greencastle, Indiana
April 8, 1930
Dear LeNore:

Again I am here working away, and it is now past 11 o'clock. And now for a few minutes with my dear one even though it is at a late hour.

I received a call to go directly to Greencastle this morning, and here I sit in this hotel when I had planned on being in Indianapolis so that I could have read my dear one's letters.

I am sure tired out tonight for the worry today almost got me. I rented a farm that was sold, and the tenant was working in the fields, and the buyer stopped him, and then he called on me, and this is another story.

Just one thing after another. You just keep going and do your stuff, and it always turns out nicely after all, regardless of how dark it may be at the time. Tomorrow will be a big help to me if the weather is good. Then I can get caught up in my territory.

I am just wondering what you have done next since standing out in the cold, cold world. Don't give the patient the wrong medicine as you know the results, and you are still running about fifty percent on deaths.

Well, dear, I am just sawing wood and working away anxiously to have each day come for it means that soon the Buick will be arriving home.

Nite, nite, dear

Always just Carl

Hotel Courtland
Kokomo, Indiana
April 15, 1930
Dear LeNore:

Arrived here rather late and pretty much tired out. Today was rain mostly, and then this evening it turned cold and very disagreeable.

I left the office rather late and then lost considerable time at Judge Cook's office in trying to get some information. I sure felt like ten hours of sleep can readily be appreciated. How can you get ten hours of sleep with so much work and driving to do?

Wondering how you are feeling this evening and if you received your long-awaited call for another case. No doubt you are getting anxious for I can just imagine waiting a long time would almost kill me.

I left the folks all well, and my baby waving bye-bye at me. She gave me a good hug and kiss before I left.

I have been thinking all day about the different conversations that we had and especially one that I have given considerable thought.

You can call the folks and tell them just where you are going, and then I can call you when I get home.

Well, dear, I must get to bed and be ready for the morrow.

Sincerely,

Carl A. Enz

Always Carl

Indianapolis, Indiana
April 25, 1930
Dear LeNore:

Now at the Claypool Hotel and taking the time this morning to answer your letter. I was sure glad to hear from you and to know that you got back into the hospital without much trouble. I am sure busy now and driving very hard each day. In fact, I have averaged 300 miles each day so far since starting the new work.

This work is fine but no results because the farmers are busy in the fields and do not care to buy until fall. I think we are making a serious mistake in working them so hard because we may lose them before fall. All I can do is follow Bill's instructions and continue making more expenses and mileage on the Buick. Feeling fine and working hard. I may be home over Sunday, hope so.

Just a traveling man,

Carl A. Enz

JAMES H. ROBINSON
PROPRIETOR

ANDERSON'S
LEADING HOTEL

THE
HOTEL STILWELL
EUROPEAN PLAN
CAFE
IN CONNECTION

Courtesy

Service

FAMOUS FOR THE QUALITY OF FOOD

ANDERSON, IND,

April 29 1930

Dear LeNore;-

Now at the above place as busy as an old
hen with 46 chickens and the heavy rains causing them
to look for shelter.   Today was a busy day for me since
my work is locateing local agents for our future land
sales.   This work is good one day and then the next day
every thing is all wrong .   Especially when every one is
gone and you can't finish one single thing.

We certainly had plenty of moisture today
and in spells.   Several of the tenants just got up to
the house when it stopped raining and they were just
drowned and the joke was good for I could say what are
you doing up here, are you working to day ? Good joke.

The Buick is working hard to make the money
that she lost for me when the springs were broken. One
can appreciate driving this kind of car and rest as you
drive.   Vance is sure under the weather and about down
because of driving the Ford and almost killing himself
before he realize the trouble.

I am feeling much better and enjoying the
work fine.

Always Carl

JAMES H. ROBINSON
PROPRIETOR

ANDERSON'S
LEADING HOTEL

THE HOTEL STILWELL
EUROPEAN PLAN

CAFE IN CONNECTION

Courtesy

Service

FAMOUS FOR THE QUALITY OF FOOD

ANDERSON, IND,

Wonder what you are doing and were you are at this
evening. No doubt that man Philips is trying to see
just how the Ford is running. HA HA,

How is Lesh and Fatty ? also Dollars and g.
Well the roads have been real good all week. HA HA.
Did you get the blinds all up before retiring.?-
We are going right straight north and we arrived at
Decatar Indiana. Seems rather strange.

Working my way south to the Claypool Hotel
and later down south th the different places that I
told you about. Very anxious to read one of you good
letters again since we are separated again.

Have you seen anymore lights on the roads
to scare you. I have passed several on my way to the
hotels at night . The warm nights brings friends
close together. HA HA.

Well dear I must continue work as usual and
try and get results in the field. Keep busy dear
and always remember that there is someone thinking
about you as days go on and soon the two weeks will
roll around for us.   ALWAYS

Carl A Enz

65

Claypool Hotel
Indianapolis, Indiana
May 1, 1930
Dear LeNore:

Just got back from the famous Hamrack Ranch south of Indianapolis. Had a very busy day today and found a few prospects for a fall sale. Appointed several good agents that will help me make a good sale.

The room just across from me tonight is somewhat of a wild place. There are two couples in there, and the booze is mighty strong. Their conversations certainly sound like they are in for a big night.

One certainly can imagine a lot when you hear the noises from just across the wall. Several bottles are sitting on the stand, and they are drinking every few minutes.

Sure hope they get tired out soon for I must have my rest. I can't get it if I must listen to them carrying on all night.

I was so anxious for a letter here at the Claypool Hotel, and when I arrived, there was none to be had. I get so lonesome here and away from the baby and my dear one and to think that I have the whole week to wonder about before I can get back home.

No letter from anyone and that means no news and plenty of blues. If I felt like this when I am at home, the insurance company would be getting another man soon. Hope you have another case immediately so that everything will go along smoothly, and you will not get so lonesome. Maybe you are not so?

Work and plenty of it are all I have in sight for the next few weeks. Wish that I could see you this evening and have a nice drive and a good old-fashioned visit.

Always Carl

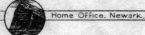

Always Carl

The Prudential
Insurance Company of America

Edward D. Duffield, President   Home Office. Newark, N

IN RE

MORTGAGE LOAN DEPARTMENT

JOHN R. McMAHON, Property Inspector
305-306 CARROLL BUILDING
FORT WAYNE, IND.   May 4 1930

Came to me wrinkled - & wadded up.

Dear LeNore;-

      Now at the Grand Hotel at Vincennes Indiana awaiting your long looked for letter and at this time do not have one single word from any one except the folks and I called them last night about eleven oclock. I drove very late last night to get down here so that I could write a few letters today and then be ready to work monday morning so that I can get the work ot out and be on my way north to good old Ft Wayne.

      What a hot room today, the windows all up and all that I can do is sit here and swet and work. This afternoon I am planning on driving out to two farms and finish them while there and then that much will be done towards a finish job in this section.

      I am wondering what you are doing today and what a chance to go out and if you have forgotten all about me and went stepping. No doubt in my mind but what you have over stepped the promises because the mating season is now on and I realize with me away out here and out of your life for the present time and the the chance for Dollars and cens to make a date for you and then laugh at me.

      I am sure blue today and certainly feel that something is doing it away back in the little city of Ft Wayne. You can rest assured that I am just working away and doing the whole thing for the future pleasue of someone who will be true to me when I am away down south and going through a terrible punishment because if you co ld only realize the punishment that goes over one so far from his only dear ones that are left for

67

The Prudential
Insurance Company of America

Edward D. Duffield, President   Home Office, Newark, N.J.

IN RE

MORTGAGE LOAN DEPARTMENT
JOHN R. McMAHON, Property Inspector
305-306 CARROLL BUILDING
FORT WAYNE, IND.

the future pleasures that will enclude many days of tried labor .

The music down below has raised me up so that I can just see over the top but I am still down in the gutter. I have about all the work out for the past week and now must plan the next weeks work and try and make a few sales before I fail in the work.

The music down below is getting me ready for dinner and I guess it is past dinner now. The Sundays are terrible for me away down here away from my only dear one . Now I suppose that you are almost sick of such a letter but maybe you have forgotten the Ossian farm home and how lonesome you got and how pleased you were to see someone.

I can fully realize how easy it is to forget to write when the chances with Dollars and the dates that she has to offer and the Car and everything. Well I guess it is all my fault for ask such a question for you must enjoy yourself and for me to be so foolish is another color.

Well dear it looks much like my punishment will continue for you are going to Indianapolis for several dates and at this time I will be home and you will be gone and then I will leave for Illinois and be gone for another two weeks. All that I have to say is dear have a good time and I will see you when I can. This sure hurts me but I guess one in my time and circumstances of life must endure everything that comes regardless.

My next address will be in care of Mathus Land Carmi Illinois No doubt but you will be busy in the next few days and weeks , I am just wondering if you will ever write to me , remember one long week and no lette blues and plenty.   Wonder what is next for me?

Just a travelling Salesman

This two-page letter had likely been wadded up.

Always Carl

The Prudential
Insurance Company of America

Edward D. Duffield, President   Home Office, Newark, N.J.

IN RE

MORTGAGE LOAN DEPARTMENT

JOHN R. McMAHON, Property Inspector
305-306 CARROLL BUILDING
FORT WAYNE, IND.   May 6 1930

Dear LeNore;-

     I am one of the men that is certainly down on women tonight. here I am away down here at a little Hotel at Carmi Illinois awaiting a letter and the thing that hurt me so bad is after I told you just were that I would be and then you were just to busy to even write to me.

     Well I am just the many men that are good enough to be aroud at a sick time and to run trips and be of help while at home and then just as soon as I am out of sight there is some one more important. I drove hard to get here this evening and then rushed down to Mr Lands and he said that there was no mail.

     Your know LeNore that I have always been kind to you and help you while you were sick and took you places and now to be forgotten so soon is almost believeable. Well this is my last letter until you answer the four that I have written.

     JUST A TRAVELLING SALESMAN,

Carl A Enz
1821 Alabama Ave
Fort Wayne
Indiana

FORECLOSURE AND
FORECLOSED PROPERTY SECTION

REAL ESTATE LOAN DEPARTMENT

ARCHIBALD M. WOODRUFF, VICE-PRESIDENT
LESTER E. WURFEL, ASSISTANT SECRETARY
R. R. ROGERS, ASSISTANT SECRETARY
JOHN F. MYLOD, ASSISTANT SUPERVISOR
F. W. McGINNIS, FIELD MANAGER

THE PRUDENTIAL INSURANCE COMPANY
OF AMERICA

EDWARD D. DUFFIELD, PRESIDENT

HOME OFFICE, NEWARK, NEW JERSEY

May 13 1930.

Dear LeNore;-

Just arrived at the Stilwell Hotel at Anderson Indiana and
have my supper and now for a few minutes with this machine. Tried hard
to make a deal today but it just seems that we are not getting results
and the land business is mighty dull.

This morning was another sad one for me at home for Donna
Ruth was pretty sick last night and her daddy was no better and this morning
found both of us in a bad way. Donna Ruth held on so tight for me and
looked so pitiful and soon the tears had to come for both of us.

Mrs Mahler has certainly found her little granddaughter
thinking considerable of her daddy and home. She is well satisfied amd
has began to realize that it would be impossible to ask for the baby after
watching the feeling this morning.

Nothing was said about the time that I came home on Sunday
evening and I did not mention it either. I wish that you could find time
to visit the folks during the week and have a nice visit with Mrs Mahler.

I am sure going to bed early this evening and try and get
over the sick spell before I get another mess at some of these fine eating
places. It sure made a sick baby out of me and has stayed with me for a
good long time.

Well dear I hope you have another case that will be off when
I get home on next Sat. evening. I believe that I am getting the Mumps ?.
Can you notice my voice.   I must get to bed soon dear, NITE NITE DEAR.

Feel much better this evening,   *Carl*

Always Carl

The Prudential
Insurance Company of America

| Edward D. Duffield, President | | Home Office, Newark, N.J. |

IN RE

MORTGAGE LOAN DEPARTMENT

JOHN R. McMAHON, Property Inspector
305-306 CARROLL BUILDING
FORT WAYNE, IND.   May 14 1930

Indianapolis

Dear LeNore;-

    Now at the Claypool Hotel and mighty busy meeting several Real Estate Men in the listing of our farms for sales purposes. Your letter did not come and I am again wondering what it is all about but this time I am coming home in one week so the time will soon be over and then I can drive home and quarrel again with you. I am sure that you letter will be in the morning mail for it will take just about that long to get around.

    I am sure that you will write me this time for the time and later quarrels are certainly trouble to me especially when I have so many other things to think about and then Mrs Mahler at home and the baby being sick and everything is enough for one person.

    Sales are mighty slow with me but one just must keep on going and trying to sell regardless of condition and surroundings. The Buick is just working fine and this is a big help towards making the day more happy. It is sure cold here this evening and I am down here without a coat and the heater taken off of the Car.

    Your really should be here and keep me warm for the rest of the week . I would call the folks but I have forgotten there name and no. I suppose Katie is taking care of a man somewhere in this country. Soon Dollars will be taking care of her Mike maybe she is doing it now?? Well dear feeling much better this evening and hope to get you letter to-morning to help start the day right. Must get busy---.

    Hope that you can get away on Sat. evening.

    NITE NITE DEAR,

Carl A Enz

FORECLOSURE AND
FORECLOSED PROPERTY SECTION

REAL ESTATE LOAN DEPARTMENT

ARCHIBALD M. WOODRUFF, VICE-PRESIDENT
LESTER E. WURFEL, ASSISTANT SECRETARY
R. R. ROGERS, ASSISTANT SECRETARY
JOHN F. MYLOD, ASSISTANT SUPERVISOR
F. W. McGINNIS, FIELD MANAGER

THE PRUDENTIAL INSURANCE COMPANY
OF AMERICA

EDWARD D. DUFFIELD, PRESIDENT

HOME OFFICE, NEWARK, NEW JERSEY

May 15 1930

Anderson, IN

Miss Le Nore Hoard

Dear LeNore;-

      Changed my trip some while working around Anderson and at
this time have stayed here at the Stilwell Hotel and plan on driving north
tomorrow and arriving at the Uncles by evening and staying with him over
night and then working my way back home by the evening.

      It is sure cold here this evening and I am still here without
my coat and must continue without it. Any way I did not start out with a
straw hat and I can see several that are wearing them.

      Came back through Indianapolis and found your letter there
at noon today. If it had not been for the trip back through the city I
would be without another week but your letter was right this time.

      Tried hard to close a $100000.00 deal but can't close it
at this time. This would be a big deal for me and I sure hope that I can
make it.

      The roads have been fine all week-- No Yes Ha. ?.........

      Feeling real good this evening considering the punk
deals that I have been trying to revive for a sale.

      Just turned on the warm water and will let the tub fill
up for a big swim before I retire. You had better go swimming with me ☺?
Hope your side is getting better for this has worried me a lot and now
it is getting worse and should be getting better by this time. Maybe
the trip to Indianapolis has started the whole thing over again.

Always Carl

REAL ESTATE LOAN DEPARTMENT

ARCHIBALD M. WOODRUFF, Vice-President
LESTER E. WURFEL, Assistant Secretary
R. R. ROGERS, Assistant Secretary
IRVING J. DENTON, Supervisor
HAROLD D. RUTAN, Assistant Supervisor
WILBUR A. CLAFLIN, Assistant Supervisor
WILMER C. VAN DUYNE, Assistant Supervisor
ARTHUR M. SEITZ, Assistant Supervisor
(Essex County Branch Office)
ERNEST H. TRACY, Assistant Supervisor (Farm Loans)
JOHN F. MYLOD, Assistant Supervisor (Foreclosures)
LOREN D. COLON, Manager
RENE J. DUFOURD, Assistant Manager

**THE PRUDENTIAL INSURANCE COMPANY
OF AMERICA**

EDWARD D. DUFFIELD, President

HOME OFFICE, NEWARK, NEW JERSEY

May 21 1930

Dear LeNore;-

Now at the Plaza Hotel at Danville Illinois with Mr Hoover
of the Straus Bros Gang. We are both at the same work and I am charging
5½ % interest and he is charging 6% and his land is $50.00 higher than
ours. We both had a good laugh about it and just go on with out work.

I had planned on writing you last night but Hoover kept me
up rather late and tried to find out more about the Company. I know
more about the Company than he does and he is working for them at the
present time.

I am going to Paxton Illinois today and try and drum up
some business for the Company. The roads are sure fine and the Buick
is doing her stuff and every day.

How are you feeling and have you girls went over to see
Mrs Mahler and my big girlie. She would be glad to have you come and
have a good visit.

I have thought about some of the stories and a good
laugh always comes. I hav'nt picked up any women along the road and
futher more will not....

Well dear I am sure wishing for more time so that I
can get some letters wrote to the office and plan my work.

Dear I must go to work for Hoover is down stairs.

BYE BYE

Carl

Hotel Orlando
Decatur, Illinois
May 27, 1930
Dear LeNore:

Received a call to meet Snyder here at 11 this morning so he will probably be here anytime. I am very anxious to see him for I think there is something good or bad and I would be disappointed if they failed me.

Drove over here mighty fast and certainly feel the effects. Tired out and not rested yet. Need a nurse.

Suppose Mrs. Mahler is on her way home in very deep sorrow, but we must all share in these sorrows sometimes in life.

Wonder what you are doing and if you are still on the same case?

Certainly will feel better after today is over.

Bye, dear

Carl A. Enz

Terre Haute House
Terre Haute, Indiana
May 30, 1930
Dear LeNore:

Away down here at this beautiful little hotel thinking a great deal and wondering what it is all about to be punished so terrible and then working so hard to make good. I am leaving early for Indianapolis to meet a good prospect at the Claypool Hotel and show him several farms west of Indianapolis and then try and close him.

I am wondering if you by chance could be so kind as to make the trip down to Indianapolis and visit your Aunt[23] over the weekend since you had planned on the trip some time ago.

No doubt at this time you were mighty busy putting away the pennies for the old age that will creep up on us sometime within the next 50 years. Suppose you have another gentleman patient as the usual. Ha. No neck trouble.

Has Miller got the right insurance on her wooden leg? Don't pay too much for that because remember you can always get reduced rates. Ha.

How glad I would be to find you waiting for me to drive out down at your Aunt's at Indianapolis when I get over there tomorrow.

Tonight I made a check up on my change and found myself about broke, and nobody knows me here. I hope I will have enough until I can get down to Greencastle, Indiana.

Wonder if you forgot about me over Decoration Day and stepped out for it was such a good day and for me to be away down here and to keep my dear all penned up in the hospital for three weeks is also considerable punishment. But what else can I do only just work hard and keep my mind off the thoughts of home?

All the students are getting back from school, and I always think of one regardless of how much you scold me for he is so hot on your trail. Someone was so good to tell me some

---

[23] LeNore's Aunt LeNore Hoard Allen, for whom she was named, lived in Indianapolis. She was one of Kellis Hoard's sisters.

more news that always comes back. You will remember that you told me that news "always comes back," but I just don't believe this until after I talk to you.[24] I think someone is interested in and is trying to do something that is not so good.

Well, dear, I wish you were here this evening so I could go to the show and have a good time instead of working continually.

Hope to see you next week if I can get home if the land men started over there.

Bye, bye, dear

Unsigned

FIREPROOF
250 ROOMS WITH BATH
RATES FROM $2.50

TERRE HAUTE HOUSE
E. L. WENZEL, PRESIDENT
TERRE HAUTE'S LARGEST AND FINEST HOTEL
WABASH AT SEVENTH STREET
TERRE HAUTE, INDIANA

---

[24] Reference to her former beau, Porter, who was in law school.

Always Carl

June 3, 1930
Dear LeNore:

No doubt you are one sore little girlie because I failed to write you over the weekend, but after you hear the trip and my experience in the past few days and all my troubles, maybe you will forgive me and come to my rescue.

Received a call from McMahon to meet an attorney at Sullivan, Indiana, and serve several ditch notices on Thursday of last week, and of course, I drove south and finished all the work and later drove up to Terre Haute and found your letter that was written several weeks ago.

Saturday morning, bright and early I started for Indianapolis against the traffic that was coming from the races[25] and indeed found driving very difficult at times. Arrived at Indianapolis at just 8:30 a.m. and found my prospect awaiting for a long ride. We drove out to his mother's place and loaded my car full of kids and the old folks, including the grandmother. We waited for one more, that was the grandfather. After he looked over the crowd, he decided to stay home!

I showed them every farm that they said they wanted to see and got home at 10:30 that evening. I got to bed at 11:30 that night, and only drove 324 miles!

They were to come Sunday morning, so I got up bright and early and got my car out and here they came and informed that they had decided to drive home and would probably come back later to buy a farm. This made me mighty sore but could not say one single word, so I looked for your letter and failed to get one, and this had me peeved, and away I went to Salem, Illinois.

I arrived late that evening and had covered 234 miles, and your letter failed to come here. The next morning I came to work slightly down in the mouth but got busy and sold a farm. The next day I sold another one, and that evening your letter came with very little news

---

[25] The 18th running of the Indianapolis 500 at the Indiana Motor Speedway was May 30, 1930. While he doesn't mention it, a cousin of Carl's, Roy Grugel, was employed by the track in the early days.

only to mention the fact that you were on the go all the time and too busy to find the time to write.

Now I am here at Danville, Illinois, at the Plaza Hotel, and still wondering what you are doing or thinking. Sometimes I wonder if I am a bore to you, and then I ask you to come out to the house and visit with Mrs. Mahler, and you finally ask her to come to the hospital.

She did not say one word on the trip up and back but acted peculiar the rest of the time that I was around her, leaving an impression that you did not care to meet her or the baby. I sure hope that I am wrong and can see it in a different light.

I would have written to you before, but I received a nice infection on my chin from a barber in Paxton, Illinois, and have suffered some lately. It has spread over my face, especially after shaving. I went to see a doctor, and he gave me some medicine that was just like fire and took all the pep out of me for the rest of the day.

My whole face was one scab but looks much better now and has stopped hurting and is healing up in excellent shape. (page missing).

Always Carl

Claypool Hotel
Indianapolis, Indiana
June 18, 1930
Dear LeNore:

Just came in from a very disappointing day in the field. Prices are terrible, and so are land prospects.

McMahon and Snyder are meeting me here tonight, and we are to go over the future work and try and get results.

The convention is over, and I am sure glad for sleep is what I need badly. No noise tonight!

Don't know what my plans are for the week and until the orders are given tonight.

Try and send you my address as soon as possible. Send your letters to this hotel, and my forwarding address will be with them later.

Hope you are feeling well. Must go for the bags are here now.

Bye, dear

Carl A. Enz

The Prudential
INSURANCE COMPANY OF AMERICA

EDWARD D. DUFFIELD, PRESIDENT   HOME OFFICE: NEWARK, N.J.

MORTGAGE LOAN DEPARTMENT

IN RE

JOHN R. McMAHON, PROPERTY INSPECTOR   *Indianapolis*
305-306 CARROLL BUILDING
FORT WAYNE, IND.   June 18 1930

Dear ·LeNore;-

    Your letter came to me this morning just as I was leaving
the Hotel and the sad part of it all is that you lost your patient and
then to the questions ask and the way that you had to answer them.

    I hurried back this evening and expected to meet McMahon
and Snyder and found a telephone call saying that I should call the
FtWayne Office and believe me It did not take me long for I was just
sure that some ome was sick.

    McMahon stated that he would be here tomorrow evening
and then we could go over the detailed report and get a clear under--
standing of the whole business.

    I forgot to write you in pencil but it is to late now
for I just kept on writing after finishing my work, but will write you
in pencil the next time that I write you.

    Mc Mahon is feeling bad because Snyder is sitting so
close on the job and seemed worried about it, maybe I will be worried
after tomorrow night and maybe they are satisfied with my work.

    I will not mention my SYMPATHY boy tonight for he ------
well it is all up to you in just what happens to him and just what he
does after you tell him just were he stands in the light.

    Just aalled the folks and found all of them well and
my baby feeling fine. Mrs Mahler wrote that we had an offer of $150.00
per Acre for our (90Acres) in Kansas and I believe that I will sell it.

    Now for a good bath and plenty of sleep for this one.

Bye Bye Dear   Carl a Enz

Carl Enz and LeNore Hoard, July 4, 1930, Van Wert, Ohio.

Note the American flags on the car.

Dixon, Illinois
July 8. 1930
Dear LeNore:

Now at Dixon, Illinois, waiting for Mr. Newcomer to go to Basco, Wisconsin. It sure looks like rain at this time and may spoil the day for us.

Drove 310 miles yesterday and may drive 250 today. Feeling fine after one good night's sleep. Last night found me ready to go to bed after 6 o'clock.

Left all the folks feeling well except Quincy and he was mighty sick last night. Kept everyone busy to keep this boy alive.

Wonder what you are doing today and tonight. Be careful of the car salesman and his future rides. Ha. I know just what you are saying and doing because I know you well enough now, don't I? Well, Mr. Newcomer is here, and we must be going so good luck to you and hope you can get a sick one.

Always Carl

Always Carl

Grand Hotel
Vincennes, Indiana
July 15, 1930
Dear LeNore:

I arrived here at 6 o'clock this evening and found your letter awaiting me. Another very good day for me because we just sold another farm for $100 per acre with $1500 down. Boy, how glad!

Tomorrow I am trying hard for another deal and maybe four for this week. Not so bad for me all alone, fighting a lone battle against odds. I can do it if anyone can. And results are in line, more each day for I am building as I go.

Starting back home tomorrow evening and plan on being home for Friday to show a prospect a farm near Fort Wayne.

Sure hope you are well again and at home getting the rest that you sure need.

Well, rest dear, your old man is out and gathering the corn for a nest egg.

Bye, dear,

Just Carl A. Enz

July 25, 1930

Dear LeNore:

Now at the hotel at Rockville, Indiana, and just about ready to leave. Sold one farm yesterday and prospects of selling one today. Sure hope so for my fame is getting weaker.

Wonder how you are this morning? Sure hope that you are feeling better for you were mighty sick Sunday evening. I stopped at a service station and got my car cleaned out for this heat certainly had me about ready to throw up.

Tried hard to locate McMahon last night for three hours and finally located him and got the whole thing over. He seemed in good humor and did not say one word about me coming home.

Left Donna Ruth feeling fine but crying mighty hard when I left. She seems to enjoy going with me and insists mighty strong.

We certainly had a wonderful Sunday evening. Ha. I will come with half a dozen handkerchiefs next time. How much would I like to go home and find you all over the blame thing, for it sure worried me to have you sick so much? Going to Vincennes, Indiana, today and then working my way back to good old Fort Wayne maybe Friday evening.

Always Carl A. Enz

September 3, 1930
Dear LeNore:

Now at Marion, Indiana, waiting on the nice rain to get settled so that I can go out and enjoy the weather. I worked with Mr. Little at the office until 11 o'clock on Sunday evening. Sold the Mahoney 80 acres north of La Fontaine, Indiana, and tried hard to sell the farm near Alexandria, Indiana.

I wonder where you are today and where you went on Sunday evening?

I left Donna Ruth feeling fine and the rest of my folks all well. Suppose you are busy cutting corn and feeding the pigs and mowing the lawn, etc.?[26]

I will be going to work soon again, so be good, dear, and watch your steps around Columbia City. Ha.

Bye, dear

Always Just Carl

---

[26] He speaks with great irony here. LeNore was not a fan of farm work.

The Hotel Stilwell
Anderson, Indiana
September 16, 1930
Dear LeNore:

I'm waiting on a call that I have for you this evening, but they tell me that you are out for the evening and I am again wondering what is it all about?

You know what I am doing this evening, working as usual (wrote 10 letters to prospects and made out my reports for the day and answered several telephone calls, and the night is almost gone. I enjoy this work when business is good. I go down mighty deep when business is poor.

I sold one farm and have prospects of selling more. I called the folks and found all of them well, and my baby feeling fine.

You have my address, but I guess you have lost it as far as I am concerned for they have failed to give me a letter thus far.

Last Sunday night was mighty long for me, and this week and next will be much longer. Your previous conversation of going away sticks in my heart. You are surely punishing me by not writing. I wonder if you have decided to quit me.

I am sitting here wondering so many different things. Your last conversation and your actions certainly have me sick. I am working so hard so I will not think so much.

Just a widower, Carl

Always Carl

September 19, 1930

Dear LeNore:

At Danville, Indiana, for the night. I sold two farms this week, and plan on selling one tomorrow. I called the folks and found them all well. I sure have the blues tonight.

My baby will be two years old soon, and the thoughts are coming back on me here. I am working hard and saving for who? Just a widower.

No letter since I left home and I don't believe that you are planning on writing to me. I wonder if you really are. I just have the blues so bad that I can't think or write.

I hope you can see some of my troubles.

Just a mere widower,

Carl A. Enz

Sullivan, Illinois
September 21, 1930[27]
Dear LeNore:

This has been one of the longest days that I have experience for some time.[15] I worked all morning, had dinner with the loan inspector, and played golf with the president of the bond company. He was a big, fat man, so I could follow him easily.

I came back and copied several loan inspections and finished all my work and now came to the place where I feel at ease. I called my folks and found them all well, and my baby enjoying her presents so much.

Thanks, LeNore, for the presents. Mrs. Mahler sent so many things. The worst thing of it all, here I am away out here. Ruth[28] certainly must have forgotten all about my girlie but she was her sponsor and should have remembered her. Maybe she intends doing my stunt of one week late.

I sure hope I can have some good sales this week and make a good showing in the section. Nothing has been done thus far.

I wonder where you are this week and tonight. You know I have always believed in you, but the old feeling of Porter on your section and me out here always comes before me.

I feel sure that you can offer a place for every evening while I am gone. But if you are going out, remember the happening at South Whitley. Somehow I feel that you are out with someone this evening.

Let's talk about something else. If I could only be home and then I could see you and not sit here and grieve.

You know, dear, just two years ago tonight I went through an experience that was certainly heart-breaking. The tears are coming freely, and the picture is here before me. I sure hope that I may never experience this again.

---

[27] Anniversary of Alma's death, and Donna's second birthday
[28] Ruth Arnold was Alma's best friend at Valpo as well as Donna's baptismal sponsor

Always Carl

I know how you feel toward me, and I am sorry that I talk this way, but dear, I sure get plenty of blues away from home and no mail from you all week. Dear, I am just wondering if you are sore at me.

Sure wish that I could get one letter from you. Dear – what is the matter?

Always Carl

The National Inn
Sullivan, Illinois
September 22, 1930
Dear LeNore:

I received your special letter this evening and sure glad, for this has been the only letter for one whole week.

I just received a call from Fort Wayne and called back and failed to find anyone at home. May stay here for two weeks and may go home tomorrow.

Sold one farm today and have three more pending that may develop into sales sometime. Mr. Little has been going with me and is sure good company and a jolly good fellow.

The territory is sure a sick one over here and is surely in need of someone to try and build it up and sell a few farms. I believe that I can move some of them if given the time and help in the territory.

No doubt you are enjoying your stay at home and at the same time getting your rest and visiting with your mother.

The folks are sure friendly to you after taking you to Lima and giving you such a nice visit. Enjoy yourself now for you can never tell; look at me now and my circumstances.

Dear, remember that I am away out here and enjoy a letter. We sure give today a good working and may do likewise tomorrow. Remember, dear, I am away out here and thinking of you always. Regards to the folks.

Your Carl

Always Carl

Plaza Hotel
Danville, Illinois
September 24, 1930
Dear LeNore:

Received your three letters, one from Crawfordsville and the other two sent here. I really did have the blues after one whole week and no mail.

McMahon asked me to drive over here and meet a prospect, and at this time nobody has come, maybe he will not arrive. It is sure raining hard here currently.

I drove over here last night and sure experienced a rough drive after nights on the farm. Just a good thing the tires did not go down on the way. The Illinois roads are terrible today, and, I may not go because of the impossibility.

The continual slump in the grain markets has toppled the whole sales program. I just can't keep prospects interested.

Wonder where you are tonight and where you will be on Saturday night? Walter is coming home, so you had better get him another date. May play golf on Sunday morning. I hope you are feeling better and not sawing wood.

Always Carl A. Enz

October 9, 1930
Dear LeNore:

Now at Anderson, Indiana, and no letter from you. I am sure that you have been kidding me.

I met McMahon here Tuesday night, and last night I talked until 10 o'clock on a deal for one of our farms. The woman was boss and certainly made a deal impossible. Have sold four farms this week and surely plan on selling more.

My cold is much better now, and I feel much more like getting out and making results. We had rain every day this week, and the fields are so muddy and grass mighty wet for someone with a bad cold.

I wonder where you are this evening. You sure have me guessing, and the only way to forget the dates that you have had is to work like the devil. That is what I plan on doing for I cannot think too much about it. You know that I have been true blue, and I am asking you. Have you?

Maybe you are doing this to punish me or for a purpose. Who knows? I must continue to try to make a success for someone.

I may be home before you get this letter, or I may be called to Illinois. You sure have punished me enough in your promise and then stepping out. You know just how I feel.

Yours for success, Carl

Always Carl

Terre Haute House
Terre Haute, Indiana
October 14, 1930
Dear LeNore:

Now at the above place and mighty glad to be here because my throat is something terrible. Last night I was so tired and sick. This morning I am feeling much better.

Going to Vincennes and then to Illinois. I hope your cold is better, for I have suffered terribly. I sure hope the baby doesn't get it.

Had a bad day yesterday but hope to have better results today. Hope you are home at Fort Wayne as we have a hard winter ahead of us (ha). Well, dear, enjoy your work, and I will see you the last of this week.

Bye dear, Carl

Crawfordsville, Indiana
November 4, 1930
Dear LeNore:

Now at the above place and mighty busy getting today's work out. I left your place and drove to Noblesville and sold our Caldwell 80 acres near Logansport, Indiana.

Tomorrow will be one long day for I have two loan inspections near here and then the long trip south. Sure will be glad when this southern work will be over.

I am sure going to spend every minute of the day on cleaning up these inspections.

After arriving at the Hoard home and found my dear one busy as usual and not going with me, well, there was a lump in my throat, and it is still there. Your expression almost had the tears coming, but just imagine what your folks would think of me (crying)? There is certainly a feeling between us that can never be broken. At least that is my feeling, and I guess your expression certainly gave me the feeling.

I will write you the news tomorrow and my location. I can see your father and the results of the election. Ha.[29] Everybody is staying up tonight, but I am going to sleep.

Bye, dear (I need my overcoat)

Always Carl and Donna

---

[29] A Democrat, Kellis Hoard was likely unimpressed Senate Republicans held their majority in Congress, with the tie-breaking vote of Vice President Charles Curtis. Herbert Hoover was President.

Always Carl

November 5, 1930
Dear LeNore:

    I'm now at Vincennes with Garrett Cozine, our property inspector, and I have just now finished our work. We are planning on starting out at six o'clock in the morning and finishing southern Illinois by Saturday noon. If everything works out, I'll be seeing you late Saturday evening if possible. Made six loan inspections today and feel mighty tired at this time.

    Feeling fine over the election results[30]. Hope you are feeling well, and you can go with me on my next trip south for these trips are mighty lonesome without you.

Nite, dear, Carl A. Enz

---

[30] Carl was a lifelong Republication. (Almost all LeNore's family were Democrats.)

Stop at Recognized Hotels   *Member American Hotel Association*

HOTEL CRAWFORD
A. B. JONES & SON
CRAWFORDSVILLE, INDIANA

DEC. 10 1930

Dear LeNore;-

Arrived at this place a few minutes ago and just called Mr Little and got my work up for the evening. Sold one farm today and may sell another one tomorrow. Took care of several sore thumbs today and feel much better this evening.

The rain is pouring down here this evening and making the trip in to this city a bad drive especially in case of tire trouble. Well, no tire tro ble and here nicely seated.

This hotel is very good for one thing and that is the glad hand and the $3.00 bed that is really worth about $1.50.

Wish you were here this evening to keep me in company for I sure get so lonesome for you and then to being so badly snowed under and every thing and so many things to think about for the next year .

Wonder what you are doing this evening and how the patient is feeling. I can just picture you sitting there and thinking all about the big changes that are to take place within the next year.

Father is mighty busy working to our advantage in trying to get located and get something that I can trade in for the farm.

I have been thinking pretty much today in fact I drove five miles out of the way and had to drive back the same distances while in one of my snowed under dreams.

My dreams are rather expensive to the company for they are paying my mileage. HA. Well dear , the short visit that we had last night was short and sweet but O how I did wish for more time or have you quit the job and come over and take care of me instead.

Sure hope to be with you soon,

Your sweetheart forever,

Carl A Enz

THE SEAT OF WABASH COLLEGE AND THE HOME OF BEN HUR

1930 History

Most of the letters are from 1930, when Carl and LeNore's relationship seems to wax and wane. We hear the anger in Carl's written voice; we infer that LeNore might be petulant as well as flirtatious with others, especially her ex-beau, Porter. Will this relationship survive?[31]

❖ Americans still struggled in the yet-to-be-named Great Depression, with agriculture prices low. 1930 was the first full year of The Great Depression, and the national unemployment rate was 8.9%.

❖ President Herbert Hoover signed the Smoot-Hawley Tariff bill on June 17, which raised duties on imported goods.

❖ Two black men were lynched in Marion, Indiana, in August and justice came slowly for the loved ones of the murdered men.

❖ In India, Mahatma Gandhi and his followers marched 200 miles to the salt beds of Jalalpur to protest the British monopoly on salt.

❖ The cartoon character Betty Boop made her debut.

❖ The United States population was 123 million.

❖ The Philadelphia Athletics bested the St. Louis Cardinals four games to two in the World Series.

❖ The United Kingdom broadcast the first television picture anywhere in the world.

❖ Famous people born in 1930 included Neil Armstrong, Purdue University graduate and the first man to walk on the moon, Warren Buffet, Ray Charles, Princess Margaret, and first female Supreme Court justice Sandra Day O'Connor.

---

[31] http://www.thepeoplehistory.com/1930.html

Lincoln Tower, completed 1930, Fort Wayne, Indiana, an icon of the downtown,

photo in the public domain, Wikipedia

Claypool Hotel
Indianapolis, Indiana
January 5, 1931
Dear LeNore:

Now at the above place and mighty comfortable after working in the rain practically all day. Sold one farm today and plan on a sale tomorrow. I sure hope for good weather until I get back. I will call the folks this evening and tell them all about the news.[32] Sure hope that you are feeling better. I just had a good, warm shower and feeling fine. Sure wish you could come along on these long trips for they are lonesome.

For your dad, success –

- The 53-acre farm, two miles west and two miles north of Van Buren, Indiana, $4800, fair buildings, good land, Cecil Jackson farm.
- William Jarvick, 60 acres, 2½ miles south of Bippus, Indiana, good house, poor barns, rolling land, $3350.
- John Gugel, 50 acres, 1¼ mile northeast New Waverly, Indiana, fair house, poor farm, fair land, price $3500.
- James Fisher, 239 acres, 11 miles northwest of Columbia City, near John Van Vorst, price, $12,500, furnish some material.
- A chicken farm, 3 miles east of Claypool, Indiana, Williard Burkett, 80 acres, gently rolling and then some, $4,000, get bid, 10% give deed, 15-year loan, 3% on principal, no commissions, 5½ percent interest

Tell your dad not to sell all of them until I get to see him. Sell the chicken farm and the 239 acres near Van Vorst!   Well, dear, you can see the folks Tuesday evening and report to them. All okay? Nite, der.

Carl A. Enz

---

[32] Perhaps this is when they became engaged.

Terre Haute House
Terre Haute, Indiana
January 7, 1931
Dear LeNore:

Have certainly been one busy boy this evening. Have been writing continually since eight o'clock and have several more to write.

The prospects are getting very anxious and are after me until I get them located. Sold one farm today and hope to sell one tomorrow. Going to Anderson, Indiana, to meet an agent and close a deal if possible.

I was sure surprised when I called and found you gone. I thought maybe you were called to Fort Wayne. I just called the folks and found out about the deal on the brick house. Perhaps if you don't get mad at me again, I can get this deal closed. Ha!

Well, anyhow, we certainly had some quarrel. You did talk loud at your home; do you suppose your folks heard what was said?

I will have my house bought by the end of next week, so you can look at it and see if it suits.

Wondering if you are still angry at me. Your voice over the telephone seemed rather strange. You have me wondering again.

Well, dear, I will be seeing you on Saturday evening.

Bye, bye, dear

Just Carl

Always Carl

The Hotel Hoosier
Danville, Indiana
January 15, 1931
Dear LeNore:

Now at the above place and not feeling very well. Left the window open last night and caught cold and sure feel tired this evening.

Freezing here this evening. Have a fair room here and expect to go to bed soon for rest is just what I need.

Have sold three farms this week and plan on selling one more before I arrive home.

Wish that I could be home in Fort Wayne with you and not away down here, so lonesome and blue. I am calling home this evening and would call you if I knew just where you were this evening. Sure anxious to know about the home and everything.

Wonder what you are doing this evening and where you are. Sure wish that I could be there. Well, dear, I will be seeing you soon and can hardly wait.

Your Carl

Hotel Severin
Indianapolis, Indiana
January 28, 1931
Dear LeNore:

Just finished my work and sure plenty of it. Have sold five farms in the last two days, three of them will pass.

Worked on a deal last night until 11 o'clock and finally closed him. Then drove here and got up early this morning and worked in the office here all day. Sure tired this evening, a good bath and to bed for me.

Wondering just how you are and what your sick patient is like? My cold is better, and I am feeling better, although I am very tired. Hope you are feeling well and have a nice steady job. Call the folks and tell them and see how the little one is feeling. Night, dear, sure lonesome for you this evening.

Your Carl

Always Carl

Hotel Orlando
Decatur, Illinois
February 2, 1931
Dear LeNore:

Now at the above place and sure busy. We made several inspections and then filled them out last night. Mr. Little is feeling much better and is sure giving me a much better chance than I expected.

We drove 355 miles the first day and worked half a day and part of the night.

Wonder what you are doing now and how your patient is now?

We are selling three farms today and maybe four. I hope you are feeling better and getting things ready for the future.

Always Carl

The Prudential
INSURANCE COMPANY OF AMERICA

EDWARD D. DUFFIELD, PRESIDENT   HOME OFFICE: NEWARK, N. J.

MORTGAGE LOAN DEPARTMENT

IN RE

R. F. LITTLE, PROPERTY INSPECTOR
206-208 CARROLL BUILDING
FORT WAYNE, IND.

Feb 10 1931

Dear Le Nore.-

    Now at a little city called Rockville Indiana and just about ready for the bed and sure glad for the 300 miles has given me a terrible headache and feel about half sick. Finished my work as far as possible in this te ritory.

    The Buick has covered over 55000 miles today and runs fairly good and only needs a n w set of rings to be in good shape again, also a trade in about JUNE Ist.

    Just wrote Mrs Mahler a nice long letter and explain the future plans and everything so that she can have considerable time to think about the whole matter and adjust her plains to the future plans that we have set before us.

    Left some of the pictures with Uncle Paul Hasselbring so he could divide them amoung the relation in that community. Found considerable ice this morning on the cement and this made the trip rather slow travelling.

    Wonder just what you are doing this evening and just were you are and how you are feeling and how nice it would be for me to be near and sit and watch you work and pinch you-- ears.

    Well, dear the week is rather long but our Sat, will soon be here and then we can be together again, and make up for the past two weeks. NITE NITE DEAR,

Your Future Bed Pardner.

Carl A Enz.

Always Carl

Crawfordsville, Indiana
February 16, 1931
Dear LeNore:

Just finished my letters and thinking mighty strong of a good bath and then bed.

Had a good day on Tuesday and sold a farm today and may sell one tomorrow. Wonderful weather for February. Certainly giving us about all the breaks in the showing of land and selling it.

The Buick going strong and sure one mud boat, for the Illinois mud sure does stick. Sure glad you called back for I will sure buy the paper.

Well, dear, the weeks are long, and the 12th of April seems so far away. Wish that you could be here.

Nite, dear,

Always Carl

Plaza Hotel
Danville, Illinois
February 18, 1931
Dear LeNore:

Arrived here rather late last night after driving 340 miles and closing two deals that McConnell tried three different times and then Zimmerman and Mr. Little made one trip and all failed.

I was surprised after I found that they could be closed and have been wondering ever since why the others failed.

I feel fine this morning and going to Crawfordsville for tonight. Wonder how you are feeling and what you are doing. I can picture you sitting at the table.

I left the folks all okay. I saw Uncle Paul at Reynolds, Indiana, and he told me to bring you along on some of these trips.

Well, dear, we must try and see some more furniture soon and get new ideas.

I will see you about Friday evening at Tunker.

Your Daddy, Carl

Always Carl

Claypool Hotel
Indianapolis, Indiana
March 4, 1931
Dear LeNore:

Now at the above place and mighty busy on my reports. Having excellent luck in finding the people at home and getting results and settlements made.

Just called the folks and found them all well and wondering what is happening, so I told them rather than keeping them in suspense so long.

Wish you were here this evening. We could see some of the bargains that they have to offer. Furniture prices are very cheap here. Well, dear, I will arrive at your place about two o'clock if possible and help you with the cake.

Bye dear. I will see you soon.

Always Carl

Hotel Crawford
Crawfordsville, Indiana
March 8, 1931
Dear LeNore:

Now at the above place and just getting ready to leave for Rockville, Indiana. Worked hard all day yesterday and failed on practically everything.

Even called home last night and found that you had just left with some young folks, so I just had to go to bed without talking to you. Sure had the blues last night.

Starting out rather early this morning and hope to be some use to the company.

Wish you would call the folks and keep in touch with the house, so we know that everything is in good condition.

Wish you would get a bid on the wallpapering. Well, dear, how well I wish you were here. Rest and get ready for about three weeks.

Bye, dear, Carl

Always Carl

Hotel Crawford
Crawfordsville, Indiana
March 16, 1931
Dear LeNore:

Arrived at this place at just 9:30 p.m. and sure glad, for this has been a long day for me.

Sure hope for a better day today and maybe I can cheer up the office and make a different air.

Wish you would call the folks and try and get someone to check up and see that part of the house is left and no damage. Hope you could get someone to bid on the job of papering the house.

Well, dear, rest, and enjoy yourself for we will soon be home with our baby and new house furnishing and everything.

Going to work now. I hope you are feeling better.

Always Carl

Rockville, Indiana
March 18, 1931
Dear LeNore:

Calling you and hearing your voice has certainly made me homesick. How well I would like for you to be here with me and share the troubles with me and enjoy the good times, also.

Sold one farm today and that helps cheer up conditions.

Well, deal, there are so many things to look after and do, so we can be comfortable in our new home. Get plenty of rest and get your work done for I will be with you as soon as I can get home.

Bye, dear, going to dreamland,

Carl

Always Carl

March 25, 1931
Dear LeNore:

Now at Danville, Illinois, and busy working on deals and trying to accomplish a few things while over here. Have fun thinking all week about the different articles that we must buy soon.

Feeling good now and working hard to get back home as soon as possible. We may come home on Friday evening, and I can stay with you at that time. Well, dear, we will soon be together, and then our plans will be many, and our good times will also be many.

Certainly, be glad when we get settled in our little home on Fairfield Avenue and have our little girlie with us. Dear, rest up and don't work too hard.

Always Carl

Always Carl

1931 History

Carl and LeNore likely set a wedding date after the holidays. We do not know when they became engaged or what activities such as showers or parties led up to their April wedding date.

The world of 1931 is still in tumult with The Great Depression engulfing most of the world.[33]

- Farmers in Arkansas staged a January riot when they had no food available for their families.
- The first "Dracula" movie was released.
- President Herbert Hoover signed a bill making "The Star-Spangled Banner" our national anthem.
- Charlie Chaplin received the Legion of Honor from France.
- New York City's Empire State Building was dedicated on May 1.
- The Rio de Janeiro 98-foot statue of Christ the Redeemer was unveiled atop Corcovado Mountain as a belated monument to 100 years of independence from Portugal.
- Dupont introduced synthetic rubber.
- In a repeat performance, the Philadelphia Athletics beat the St. Louis Cardinals in the World Series, this time in seven games.
- Famous people born in 1931 included James Dean, Mohammed Ali, Mickey Mantle, Mikhail Gorbachev, Archbishop Desmond Tutu, and Toni Morrison.

---

[33] https://www.timelines.ws/20thcent/1931.HTML

On the Road

Carl stayed in many hotels throughout his career. To our knowledge, only one of these properties operates as a hotel today. The historic Omni Severin Hotel is still operating in downtown Indianapolis.

Opened in 1917 by businessman Henry Severin, the hotel is Indy's oldest luxury property.[34] It was originally known as the "Grand Hotel of Indianapolis," and was located close to Indy's Union Station to accommodate business and other travelers.

The hotel website notes that "The Omni Severin sweeps visitors back to the past with its dramatic, romantic marble staircase and breathtaking Austrian crystal chandelier located in the Severin Ballroom Lobby, both dating back to 1913."

Carl frequently met with office brass and clients in hotel lobbies. As much as he enjoyed the ambiance of the Severin and the Claypool hotels in Indianapolis, he also stayed in hotels in Danville and Mt. Vernon, Indiana, that advertised "running water" as an amenity. Anyone who has worked in sales or traveled for business can appreciate the delight of a comfortable bed and the annoyance of a cold or poor room or drunken neighbors.

The Claypool Hotel stationery reflects Jazz Age design, at the end of the Art Deco period.

---

[34] https://www.historichotels.org/hotels-resorts/omni-severin-hotel-indianapolis/history.php

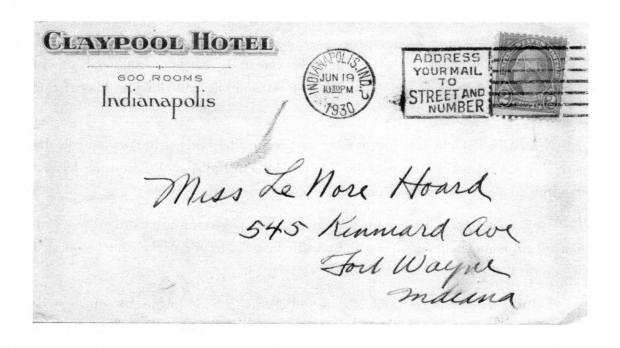

Straus Brothers and Prudential

Carl's first employer was the Straus Brothers Company, and he was employed by them for about eight years. In 1930, he joined Prudential and worked for the real estate department.

Beginning in the mid-1850s and continuing until the 1920s, Ligonier, Indiana, had a large and flourishing population of German-Jewish immigrants. Three of these early settlers, brothers Frederick, Jacob and Mathias Straus, founded the original firm of Straus Brothers at Ligonier in 1850.[35] It grew into what became recognized as the largest firm of improved farm merchants in the country.

Eventually, it became too large and successful to remain in a small, rural community in a remote corner of northeast Indiana. On July 15, 1922, the announcement was made that the Straus Brothers Co., with capital and surplus of $4 million, would move its main offices from Ligonier to the Otis Building on South LaSalle Street in Chicago.

Fort Wayne would become the new home of the real estate department, and the company would retain its interest in, and control and management of, the Citizens Bank of Ligonier and various other enterprises in which it had been engaged.

THE STRAUS BROTHERS COMPANY

ESTABLISHED 1860

FARM LANDS - MORTGAGES

ABE ACKERMAN, Pres.
JAMES I. D. STRAUS, Vice Pres.
ROBT. H. CARLSON, Vice Pres.
GEORGE M. RALSTON, Treas.
MAURICE BRUBAKER, Sec'y

HOME OFFICE
FORT WAYNE, IND.
BRANCH OFFICES
DETROIT, MICH.
CHICAGO, ILL.

FORT WAYNE, INDIANA

Some 20 years later the Straus Brothers announced the significant land acquisition in Paulding County, Ohio, east of Fort Wayne. This was an 1800-acre farm known as the Murray Grange, formerly owned by Judge Ninde of Fort Wayne, for the sum of $135,000.

---

[35] https://www.kpcnews.com/article_eef67f1b-ab76-589c-9ae1-35c9aebf17c4.html

(Charles Enz, Carl's father, worked for Straus Brothers and was also building his personal farm holdings. He purchased farms noted for rich, fertile fields in eastern Allen County, Indiana, and western Paulding County, Ohio.)

At Straus Brothers and later with the Prudential Insurance Company, Carl's activities were affected by the oncoming Great Depression. From a 2009 letter to the author from Donna Argon, "Most farmers were having a very hard time. I think that it was Carl's business to see that mortgage-holders were able to keep up payments, as well as advise farmers when they ran into trouble. He sometimes acted as an intermediary with the farmer and the company, to keep both in business.

Donna continued, "When farmers went broke, Carl let the company know when good farmland became available. The company bought the farm and put a farmer on it who could manage."

Carl demonstrated a sense of pride in his work. He was recognized by Prudential with the Old Guard award, of which he was "mighty" as he might say, proud.

PRUDENTIAL sells farms . . .

FRANK HODGSON
Agent, Decatur.

CARL A. ENZ
Property Mgr., Springfield.

GUY S. LITTLE
Farm Supervisor, Sullivan.

With Herald Review Classified

For the past three years, the Prudential Insurance Co., Illinois Branch, has depended almost entirely on Herald Review Classified to reach prospective buyers for Illinois farms listed by the mortgage loan department. That this advertising has been satisfactory is best indicated by the fact that Carl Enz, Property Manager, has been a consistent leader among all Prudential property managers in the United States. Mr. Enz and his associates believe in Herald Review "farm for sale" advertising.

You will find Prudential ads
Regularly in Classification 83

Write Classified
or Dial
5151

The Prudential Life Insurance Company. In early 1930, Carl moved from Straus Brothers to the Loan Mortgage department of The Prudential Life Insurance company. He initially worked out of the Fort Wayne, Indiana, office, and moved to the Springfield, Illinois, office in 1931. This advertisement is from the "Herald" newspaper, Decatur, Illinois.[36]

---

[36] https://www.newspapers.com/image/84695107/?terms=Carl%2BEnz

Always Carl

Family Gallery

Arrival in America. Carl's grandparents George and Amalie Weise Enz arrived in Reynolds, Indiana, from Eltingen, Württemberg, Germany in the 1860s. The latter half of the nineteenth century found many Germans coming to America.

With few resources, the young couple rented a room at the train depot in the small White County town.

Within several decades, they owned a successful farm and had raised ten children. Their oldest, Charles, was Carl's father.

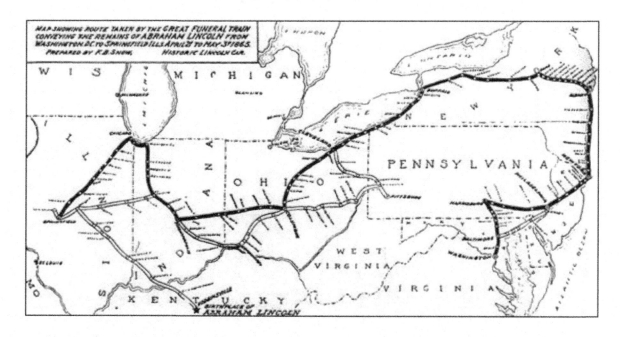

Funeral Train in Indiana. Because George and Amalie lived at the train station, they would have witnessed Lincoln's funeral train passing through on May 1, 1865, as indicated on the map above, from the Emory News Center, 2013.

Abraham Lincoln was assassinated at Ford's Theater, Washington, D.C., during a performance of "Our American Cousin" in April 1865. The county was in shock over Lincoln's death as well as the end of the Civil War. After the state funeral, Lincoln's body was placed on a special funeral train car. With an entourage of family and friends, the remains of our 16th president traveled up the coast and then west, with burial at Springfield, Illinois.

The train passed through Indiana and stopped on April 30 in Indianapolis, where the casket was displayed at the State House. The Indianapolis "Daily Star" noted for the 3:35 a.m. May 1 passing through Lafayette, "The houses on each side of the railroad is (sic) illuminated, and, as elsewhere, badges of mourning and draped flags are displayed. Bonfires blazing and bells tolling, and the people are assembled at all the stations to view the train."[37] After leaving Lafayette for a trip to Michigan City, the train passed through Reynolds early on the morning of May 1, 1865.[38]

---

[37] http://histsociety.blogspot.com/2013/03/mapping-past-roundup.html
[38] https://blog.history.in.gov/the-lincoln-funeral-train-in-indiana/

Family Photo about 1890, Reynolds, Indiana. George and Amalie Enz and their ten children. Charles, the oldest, born in 1868, was Carl's father. Charles is the tallest of the boys and in the back. He was close to his brother Gottlieb, who is nearly as tall as Charles and is in the back on the far right.

Losing Parents Early. Carl's mother, Augusta Hannaman Enz was born in Reynolds, Indiana, in 1875. Her parents died of tuberculosis when she was around four. Augusta and her younger sister, Ida, went to live with relatives. The 1880 census located the sisters in the household of Theodore Westphal, likely a cousin. Augusta's baptismal certificate lists her parent's names as Friedrika Westphal and Carl August Hannmann.

St. James Lutheran Church, Reynolds, Indiana, found this baptismal record for Carl Enz's mother, Augusta, in their records in spring 2019. While her later death certificate records her name as Hannaman, the handwritten baptismal record notes it as Hannmann, with the German markings for the double letter.

Charles and Augusta Enz, Wedding Picture, 1896

Children of John Tyler Hoard and Catherine Creager Hoard. This portrait was taken in South Whitley, Indiana, in the early 1890s and features left to right: Peter and Alice, seated; middle row: LeNore and Myrta; back row: Kellis (father of LeNore Hoard Enz), Archie, and Charles.

Kellis and Anna Long Hoard. One of two formal wedding portraits of LeNore's parent's wedding in 1898. Portrait made in South Whitley, Indiana, by Oliver Frank Kelly.

A family portrait of the Charles and Augusta Enz family, likely taken in Marion County, Ohio about 1910. Walter Henry is seated between his parents and Edith Marie and Carl August are behind their parents.

Alma Mahler with her dolls as a child in Scott City, Kansas. Alma played piano and sang at local churches, was a good student, and participated in fair activities.

Fiftieth Wedding Anniversary of George and Amalie Enz. George and Amalie pose at Reynolds, Indiana, with their ten children in 1916. Charles, Carl's father, is seated in the front row on the left.

In Scott City, Kansas, Adolf and Tillie Mahler with their daughter, Alma, who was born in 1905. Adolf died in 1916. Alma's parents came west in the 1880s as many German immigrants heard the call "Westward, Ho." Scott County, Kansas, where Adolf and Tillie became landowners, is only two counties away from the Colorado border. In Kansas, farmers don't talk about acres, but sections (640 acres.) Individual farms like the Mahlers owned were far larger than Midwestern counterparts. While Indiana farmers had adversity, the dust didn't rise in the terrible "Dust Bowl" storms of the plains.[39]

From the Kansas Historical Society, "Many factors led to the Dust Bowl. The increased demand for wheat during World War I, the development of new mechanized farm machinery, along with falling wheat prices in the 1920s, lead to millions of acres of native grassland being replaced by heavily disked fields of straight row crops. Four years of drought shriveled the crops and left the loose topsoil to the mercy of the ever-present winds."

---

[39] https://www.kshs.org/kansapedia/dust-bowl/12040

Children of Kellis and Anna Hoard, taken in South Whitley, Indiana, about 1909. LeNore is the baby, and May and Zoe flank her.

This is also another Oliver Frank Kelly portrait (noted on the part of the frame removed).

At the Tunker farm date unknown.

Kellis and Anna Hoard with their three daughters, May, LeNore, and Zoe.

Alma Mahler

Always Carl

Mr. and Mrs. F. H. Mahler

desire to announce the marriage of

their daughter

Alma

to

Mr. Carl A. Enz

on Wednesday, July the sixth

nineteen hundred twenty-seven

Scott City, Kansas

At Home
July 25, 1927
2009 Columbia Ave.
Fort Wayne, Indiana

Carl and Alma Enz at home in Fort Wayne, Indiana.

Infant Donna and her maternal grandmother, Tillie Mahler.

Baby Donna and her father Carl Enz inspecting the crops,

a favorite activity of Carl's throughout his life.

Always Carl

LeNore Hoard

Miss LeNore Hoard

and

Mr. Carl A. Enz

Request the Honor of Your Presence

at their Marriage

on Sunday the Twelfth of April

at Four O'clock P. M.

St. Pauls Lutheran Church

Barr Street, Fort Wayne, Indiana

<u>**Wedding Day.**</u> The Columbia City newspaper ran a lengthy story the next day about the Sunday, April 12, 1931 wedding. (Having worked on the Society page of the very same newspaper 50 years later, the author suspects the article was written the previous week and held until Monday.)

Zoe Hoard served her sister as maid of honor, while Walter Enz was the best man.

Kellis and Anna Hoard hosted a wedding dinner before the service at their Tunker farm for the wedding party. Donna Enz was two-and-a-half and wore a blue dress.

The article mentions that the couple left on a brief honeymoon, but doesn't indicate where.

Gottlieb Enz was a younger brother of Charles Enz by a decade. Uncle Gottlieb was a special person to Carl Enz, and they remained close until Gottlieb's death in 1949. As a young man, Gottlieb left the farm of his parents George and Amalie Enz at Reynolds, Indiana, to seek his fortune in Oklahoma. Gottlieb eventually became president of The First National Bank of Guymon. Shared by his granddaughter Leysa Enz via her late father Bob are these replicas of bills from 1929. Bank presidents signed their own money, and Gottlieb's signature is in the lower right-hand corner of the first bill.

When Alma Enz died suddenly in September 1928, Gottlieb and his wife Edith (whom he married in 1915) traveled from Oklahoma to Scott City, Kansas for her service and burial. Carl and his father, Charles, accompanied Alma's body from Fort Wayne to Kansas, while Grandma Augusta Enz stayed in Indiana with the baby.

Carl visited Oklahoma to see his uncle, and Gottlieb often visited Indiana to see family and friends in the area.

Leysa Enz Lowery, who is the daughter of Robert and Fran Enz and the granddaughter of Uncle Gottlieb, told the author this story in June 2019. "One story of Gottlieb that my father shared involved what happened after his death. People began showing up at my father's house to pay back personal loans Gottlieb had made to them. These were local farmers who had struggled in previous years and didn't qualify for bank loans. My grandfather, good-hearted as he must have been, provided loans from his personal finances to help them. And they returned the payments upon his death to my father. Dad was flabbergasted. He had no idea his father had helped so many people and that they felt honor-bound to repay the debt upon his death even though his descendants knew nothing of the amounts owed. It was a different time, but it was also a credit to the man he was. I do wish I had known him."

The Next Chapter, Springfield, Illinois

Carl Enz married LeNore Hoard on April 12, 1931, at St. Paul Lutheran Church in downtown Fort Wayne, Indiana. The new family moved to their Fairfield Avenue home for about six months until Carl took a job with Prudential in Springfield, Illinois.

Marilyn Anne Enz was born on March 28, 1932. The photo *above* is Donna and Marilyn with Grandma Tillie Mahler and LeNore Enz standing by the first Springfield house. The estimated date of the photo on the left to be summer 1933.

Donna has fond memories of living in Springfield, her elementary school building and fellow students, and neighborhood children. The family moved just a few blocks to a larger home about 1935. The picture *at right* shows Donna on the front porch of this second home, a home she dearly loved for its fireplace and spacious backyard.

These pictures were taken by the author in 2009 on a visit to Springfield, Illinois, a span of some seventy years after the images on the previous page were made.

What is immediately apparent to the modern visitor is that both owners have something decorative on the front porch and the gutters on the left side appear the same. Surely the homes have been updated.

The photo *above and to the right* is a 2009 photo of their second home in Springfield. Note that the house appears to have the same door, and possibly the same light fixture. A tiny portico has been added.

LeNore Enz's father died in 1932. Along with many farmers, Kellis and Anna had struggled to keep the farm going. Carl and LeNore, with the help of Carl's father Charles, bought Anna Hoard's and daughter Zoe Hoard's interests in the farm.[40] The farm remained in the family until 2010 because of the generosity of Charles Enz and the excellent management of Carl Enz and son-in-law William McVay.

---

[40] According to a 1933 deed owned by the author.

Carl holding Marilyn, and Donna standing, about 1933.

The Family Today

On the weekend of September 21, 2018, the family gathered in Bedford, Massachusetts, to celebrate the 90th birthday of Donna Enz Argon. Few words can describe the joy felt at the special luncheon to honor Donna, but the pictures tell it all.

<u>Front, left to right</u>: Carson McVay, Chicago, Illinois; Donna Enz Argon, Bedford, Massachusetts, and Alexander Abbott, Silver Spring, Maryland.

<u>Back, left to right</u>: Andy McVay, West Lafayette, Indiana; Amy McVay Abbott, Newburgh, Indiana; Kemal Enz Argon, Konya, Turkey; Cemal Argon, Haverhill, Massachusetts; Ahmet and Rebecca Girvin-Argon, Keswick, Virginia; Mehmet and Leeann Argon, Shirley, Massachusetts, Patrick Sheehan and Angela Argon, Haddonfield, New Jersey. Other great-grandchildren include Adam and Andrew Argon, Charles Argon, and Aziz Argon, and a granddaughter-in-law, Zeliha Üstün Argon.

Always Carl

Afterword

"Life can only be understood backwards, but it must be lived forwards."
— Søren Kierkegaard [41]

This project would not exist without my aunt, Donna Argon, who saved these letters and entrusted them to me. Aunt Donna has loved me unconditionally. She is a role model in grace to everyone lucky enough to know her.

My husband, Randy, has been listening to family stories for more than 40 years. He has given research advice, editing skills, and steered me in the right direction. He remains the love of my life, and I'm thankful I met him on the way to a college yearbook workshop at Ohio University in August 1977.

A huge thank you and shout out to Diana Ani Stokely, www.grafixtogo.com, Hamilton, Texas, who outdid herself with the beautiful cover design. She repositioned the original picture to take advantage of the beautiful Art Deco frame and extended the texture of the frame to the back cover.

She also helped me with an interior template so that I did not need to redo the pictures multiple times. I truly appreciate her patience with me and her overflowing creativity.

I am also grateful to my writer pals Dr. Mary Kay Jordan Fleming and Pam Kiser-Records, both accomplished writers, who pulled me off muddy roads and out of metaphorical ditches.

Also, I offer appreciation to:

- ❖ My first cousin, Ahmet Rauf Argon, who shared many Mahler and Enz family pictures.
- ❖ Leysa Enz Lowery, my distant cousin, for permitting me to use a copy of her grandfather's bank bills as well as sharing a story about Uncle Gottlieb.
- ❖ Elizabeth Kronewitter, Peabody Public Library, Columbia City, Indiana, for amazing discoveries for this and the next project.
- ❖ Pastor Charles Blakey, St. James Lutheran Church, Reynolds, Indiana, for finding Augusta's baptismal record (during the week of Lent, no less.)

---

[41] https://www.goodreads.com/quotes/tag/past

There's always a new project. Next: LeNore Hoard's history in Whitley County, Indiana, yet unnamed.

Several pioneering families set off for the undeveloped areas of Indiana with a team of oxen and hearts full of courage. Two men, who don't know each other, Reuben Long and Peter Creager, purchased 160-acre farms six miles apart.

Both of their ownership documents are dated August 1, 1837, from the Land Patent Office in Fort Wayne, Indiana. Both bear the duplicated signature of President Martin van Buren. Long's 160-acres are in Washington Township, Whitley County, Indiana, while Peter Creager's land is in Cleveland Township, also Whitley County, near the new town of South Whitley, then known as Springfield.

This book tells the story of pioneers who cleared and conquered a wild land, building lives and communities.

1898 Wedding of Peter Creager's great-grandson Kellis Hoard
to Reuben Long's granddaughter Anna Long at Tunker, Indiana.

The author, Amy McVay Abbott (www.amyabbottwrites.com), is one of Carl and LeNore Hoard Enz's six grandchildren and is seated second from right in this 1960s picture at Tunker. The others are Ahmet Argon, Mehmet Argon, Andrew McVay, Cemal Argon. Kemal Argon was an infant and is not in this picture.

always Carl

For More Information

My goal is everything online (or into books), so I've left a long trail for posterity. My family tree on https://www.ancestry.com/family-tree/tree/72898255/family is called "Amy LeNore McVay Abbott" and is accessible to anyone with an Ancestry account or a public library card that provides free Ancestry access.

For further research into the Enz family in Germany, our distant cousin Marc-Andre Kuhn has information at www.MyHeritage.com, also free in most libraries. Mark-Andre is a descendant of one of our patriarch George Enz's siblings.

Always Carl

Index

Made in the
USA
Monee, IL